MORGAN

From one classic
to another — enjoy, Mark!
Love,
Ruddell
Spring, 1981

MORGAN

First and Last of the Real Sports Cars

Gregory Houston Bowden

DODD, MEAD & COMPANY · NEW YORK

I.S.B.N. 0–396–06732–8
L.C.C.N. 72–5944
First published in U.S.A. 1973
Printed and bound in Great Britain by
Butler & Tanner Ltd
Frome and London

The story of the Morgan spans more than sixty years of history and for that reason it has been impossible to mention every detail. There is a wealth of information which I have either failed to discover or have discovered and been obliged to set on one side for lack of space.

I hope my many friends in the Morgan world, to whom this book is dedicated, will forgive me for its shortcomings.

G.A.H.B.
Thame, March 1972

Note to second impression

How agreeable it is to be writing a foreword to the second impression only a few months after the publication of the first! There have been a number of interesting happenings in the Morgan world since we last went to press, and so I am taking this opportunity to bring the book up to date.

In September 1972 Peter Morgan acquired the large factory next to the Morgan works in Pickersleigh Road. Since then he has let part of it cn a short-term lease while retaining 12,000 square feet. The trim shop, final finishing department, final electrical department and test shop have all been moved in there, resulting in a great improvement in the flow of cars through the factory. Mr. Morgan hopes that before long the extra space and improved flow should enable him to get nearer his target of 750 cars per year.

On the technical side, enthusiasts will be interested to know that since June 1972 the Plus-8 has been fitted with Rover's excellent new four-speed all-synchromesh gearbox, and a new back axle will be fitted from June 1973. The new axle has a ratio of 3.31 : 1 as opposed to the previous 3.58 : 1, and its effect will be to increase the top gear speed per 1,000 r.p.m. from 21.8 m.p.h. to 23.6 m.p.h. If the Rover V-8 will still hit 6,000 r.p.m. with the new axle, the car's top speed should go up to 140 m.p.h. and that will mean some very exciting motoring!

G.A.H.B.
Thame, March 1973

Acknowledgments

The author gratefully acknowledges the following for their invaluable assistance in supplying information and articles, without which it would have been impossible to write this book: The Morgan Motor Co. Ltd., Mr. and Mrs. Peter Morgan, Miss Dorothy Morgan, Mr. W. G. McMinnies, Mr. Brian Watts, Mr. Jim Goodall, Mr. Cecil Jay, Mr. Maurice Owen, *Autosport* Magazine, Mr. Christopher Lawrence, and Mr. Acock.

He also wishes to express his thanks to the Directors of the Morgan Motor Co. Ltd., Mr Brian Watts (the three-wheeler chapters) and Mr. Michael Sedgwick, for checking the factual accuracy of the text; to Sir Frank Bowden, Bt., Mr. Peter Morgan, Mr. Brian Watts, and Miss Lorna Gentry, for examining the text and proof-reading; to his brother Mr. Adrian Houston Bowden, for his good humour and patience in taking so many of the photographs which appear in this book.

Finally, he wishes to thank the following for their kind permission to reproduce photographs in this book: *I.P.C. Transport Press*, *Autosport*, *Motor Cycling*, *The Motor Cycle*, *The Motor*, *The Autocar*, *The Light Car and Cyclecar*, *The Tatler*, *The Globe and Mail*, Ed Franklin, B.I.P.S. Ltd., E. Selwyn Smith, E. G. Hodgkins, Len Thorpe, and Charles Conti. He would like to point out that as many photographs were reproduced from scrap albums, it has not always been possible to trace their source. He wishes to apologize to anyone who is not included in this list for that reason.

Contents

Illustrations

Foreword by Peter Morgan

'Looking back through the years, seeing both errors and triumphs in their correct perspective, I feel that I have enjoyed it all. The motor trade has been, as far as I am concerned, a most interesting business' – a statement made by my father, H. F. S. Morgan, during a press interview shortly before he died in 1959, and a few months before the Morgan reached its fiftieth anniversary. From my own experience, it is a summary which I whole-heartedly endorse.

During the last decade, certain writers have approached the company about the preparation of an historical record, but when confronted with the records available, particularly the information collected by my grandfather, Prebendary H. G. Morgan, all considered the task rather too great. However, during 1969 a young undergraduate from Oxford visited the factory in Malvern, and having gained certain knowledge concerning his own Plus-4 four-seater, inquired about writing a biography of the Morgan. His enthusiasm was tremendous, and he was quite undaunted by the volume of work and the amount of research which this would inevitably entail. Consequently, Gregory Houston Bowden commenced this book after completing his studies at Oxford University, which later led to a degree in Modern History.

He has collected a large amount of material from the factory and from numerous outside sources, including many individuals who have differing connections with Morgans, and rather than producing a somewhat tedious history of various models constructed over the years, he has welded together a variety of information about the company, the cars, and their owners.

One of the more frequent questions asked in regard to the Morgan is the reason for the car being built in its present style. H. F. S. Morgan set the pattern for this policy, as he personally felt that from an aesthetic point of view the long bonnet (or, with due respect to our American friends, hood), together with the sweep of the wings (or fenders) and the low overall height, was attractive to behold. This contention can be supported today by evidence of the large number of cars produced from the late twenties up until 1939 which are now recognized as classics. It will be interesting to learn whether as many post-war cars will in future years come within this respected category.

A further question sometimes arises as to how a small unit can exist in this day of giant firms. This point is commented upon in the text of the book, but due recognition and appreciation must be expressed towards all the many firms supplying the large number of items that go into the building of our cars. The interest, enthusiasm and help shown throughout the years by both the vast and the small supplying firms is very gratifying and gives us great encouragement for the future.

In conclusion, it is hoped that all who read this book will enjoy the story, and find that producing an individualistic vehicle such as the Morgan is not quite so much of an anachronism as some might believe.

P.M.
Malvern Link, June 1972

A Morgan Poem

from *The Light Car and Cyclecar*, 16th April 1926

List while I tell of the Morgan,
Its charms, its needs and its works,
The joy of trouble-free trips,
And the places where danger lurks.

Look to your rad. in the morning,
To see if the water is there,
And if it is frosty at even
To empty take every care.

Next in order, see to your oil,
To be without is a crime;
In engine sweetness you'll "XL"
If same is free from grime.

Your gearbox, steering and hubs,
Need greasy attention too,
And after each five hundred miles
Well—there's a job for you.

Occasionally, one a thousand,
Part each of your springs and grease,
Reverse the chains, oil inside clutch
And the lot will run with ease.

Don't slam the clutch into action,
Don't put oil where there's dirt.
Wipe it all off carefully
With a rag or a piece of your shirt.

Thanks for reading this nonsense
It is not written for fun.
It's just a needful reminder
For a safe and happy run.

Introduction

My own interest in Morgans began when I was seven years old. I do not know why at an age when I should have been wanting a railway engine I yearned for a Morgan, but nevertheless I did. Of course I asked my father to buy me one, but he thought that I ought perhaps to wait at least until I had learned to drive, and so I reluctantly began my long wait.

During my years at school I was just a little tempted by vintage Rolls-Royces and Bugattis, which had been my mother's dream cars as a girl, but when I went up to Oxford —still, alas, without a full driving licence—my mind was soon made up. My college was in Mansfield Road—one of the quieter corners of Oxford where the traffic wardens were less demon-like than in the centre and a favourite long-term parking place for undergraduates. At this time Mansfield Road happened to be the resting place of two Morgans; a silver and slightly battered old-style four-seater and an almost brand-new British Racing Green 4/4 two-seater. The presence of these two fine machines meant from the start that it always took me twice as long as anyone else to walk up the road, for the temptation to examine them proved irresistible every time. As I was an historian, I made occasional journeys to the History Library in Merton Street. At first I did not use the Library very regularly, but soon the frequency of my visits greatly increased when I discovered that a rather rusty, black, four-seater Morgan with wire wheels was regularly parked in Merton Street. There was something particularly appealing about this one; its tattered condition merely served to make one imagine what it must have looked like when new. It was low and sleek with a belt over the bonnet, and under the radiator grille was a distinguished number—WXA 6. I was delighted when at the beginning of my second year at Oxford I discovered that this car had also come to live in Mansfield Road. By this time, with three cars to examine, my journeys along the road were taking a long time.

I soon decided that it was absurd to spend so much time gazing at other people's Morgans and that it was high time I acquired one of my own. I therefore wrote a letter expressing my wish to buy WXA 6 and left it wrapped in a polythene bag under the windscreen wiper. The letter remained pressed to the windscreen for two or three days and then vanished, so that when I failed to receive any reply I assumed the paper had either been lost or removed by a traffic warden.

It was almost a year later that I received an envelope through the inter-college post from an American postgraduate called Tim, saying that he was returning to the States and would therefore be selling his Morgan four-seater. By this time I had almost forgotten the idea of buying the rusty black Morgan, but I realized that this must be the car to which Tim was referring. I went to see him immediately but by the time I arrived at his house he had decided to export his car to America instead of selling it in England. Fortunately, it has never been in my nature to give up without a struggle and having got as close as this on the hot scent of a Morgan, I was determined to succeed. I took Tim out to a succession of lunches during each of which I did two things: I raised my price and I tried to convince him that I would be a worthy owner of his car. Finally I came back to my rooms late one evening and found a letter informing me that I only had to write out a cheque and the car was mine.

This called for celebration and what could be better for this purpose than a drink of Malvern water? I was determined to have a ritual drink of the stuff at once to toast the beginning of my career as a Morgan-owner, but where does one buy Malvern water in the middle of the night? I changed quickly and made myself adequately presentable to go to the smartest hotel in Oxford where I bribed the night-porter to sell me a bottle. Back in my own rooms I laced the water with stronger liquids and pondered happily on my good fortune.

Now that the deal was done, all that remained was for my American friend and his wife to help me establish a really good relationship with WXA 6, and to introduce me to some of the minor hazards which accompany the many joys of owning a Morgan. One of the most obvious of these was the difficulty of climbing into the back seat when the hood was up and here my friend's wife was not too helpful; indeed, she insisted that I should look the other way as she struggled in. After a few sessions I began to feel quite at home, although I must confess that it took me far longer to understand the Morgan fully (if indeed I do fully understand it even now) than any other car. I have always been fortunate enough to have the opportunity to drive many different kinds of car from Morris Minis to Rolls-Royces and Ferraris, and in every case I have always felt fully at home with each within a few minutes of first driving it. With the Morgan it was different. If I wanted to open the window, instead of sliding it or winding it down I had to stop, unscrew it and install it under the tonneau cover in the space behind the rear seats. If I wanted to make a signal, instead of just flicking a lever on the steering column I had to swivel a switch on the extreme right of the dashboard. But it was not as simple as that, for in the first place this switch would only work if moved into precisely the correct position and secondly there was no kind of self-cancelling mechanism. I found the steering very novel and responsive—only a little turn on the wheel was needed even on a sharp bend. I found the handbrake a great delight—I do not know whether there was a Casanova in the Morgan design department at one time, but if there was, his influence can be most clearly seen in its position.

It was interesting to discover that with the Morgan there was a brand-new technique for doing everything. Climbing in and out required great dexterity and to close the doors properly was a real art. I was amused at first by the bumpiness of the suspension (for I took off from my seat three times on my first journey home), yet all this has become so normal that I now find the ride in most other cars just soggy. At first, however, the words of an American girl seemed particularly true. She told me about her Morgan which was fitted with a Selectaride control and said she greatly enjoyed choosing which of the four degrees of hard to use. The girl had in fact come to love the ride of her Morgan, and was never discouraged by those who warned her that it was the only car in which a driver could tell whether the penny he had just run over was heads or tails up.

My skill in the art of hood erection was greatly improved by a rainstorm which came on suddenly one day when I was driving along with the car open. Necessity is unquestionably the mother of invention and I quickly invented an efficient way to carry out this delicate operation. Finally, I found that with only a few days' practice it became second nature to me to press the little button on the floor which squirted oil into the front suspension and I do not think that I have failed in this duty ever since. The only hazard here is that I like to watch the oil pressure gauge fall back as I do it, and if I try to do so while driving along it can make life somewhat tricky for dogs and cyclists.

The only sad incident in the story of the forging of my

relationship with the Morgan occurred the first time I ever drove the car without its former owner. On the whole I am a law-abiding driver, but being elated by the feel of the Morgan and being restricted to a meagre 50 m.p.h. on a broad and not very busy road near Oxford, I found the temptation to go a little faster than the limit quite impossible to resist. I asked my passenger if there was a police car anywhere behind us, and when he assured me there was not, I crept up to the not very alarming speed of 60 m.p.h. One mile later I asked my passenger to look again. This time his report was less satisfactory, and a second later an infuriating two-tone horn warned me that my luck was out. The police car lurched in front of me and forced me to stop. We both climbed out.

'That's a pretty potent motor vehicle you've got there, sir,' said the policeman.

'Oh really?' said I nervously. A month later I was fined £15 and have stayed out of trouble ever since.

When I felt that I had really got to know WXA 6 I decided that it would be a good idea to have her beautifully restored, and so began a frantic period of two months during which I found myself as busy as the architect of a giant building. At this time the factory in Malvern was too busy to take in the car, and so it was essential to find coachbuilders and other specialists who could take on the work locally. I visited many firms and found that most of them fell into two categories: either they simply said they would not touch the car, or they pretended that they were willing to work on it while making it impossible for me to give them the job by quoting absurdly high estimates and telling me that they could not start work for six months. At last I found a small firm whose owner took an immediate liking to the car and so took on the job, on the condition that I would be responsible for obtaining all the necessary parts. This I readily agreed to, for I had been looking for an excuse to visit Malvern for some time and here was a perfect opportunity. I therefore rang the factory at once, ordered the necessary parts and at the same time made an appointment to meet Peter Morgan.

I found the drive to Malvern very exciting and as I crossed the border into Worcestershire I felt the same kind of exhilaration as must have been felt by crusaders when they first entered the Holy Land. However, when I finally arrived at Malvern Link station and found the turning into Pickersleigh Road, I thought something must be wrong: Malvern Link and more particularly Pickersleigh Road are places where one expects to find tennis courts and golf clubs

The Morgan factory as it is today

rather than factories making sports cars. Happily I was not
lost, for there, looming up in front of me at the end of
Pickersleigh Road, was a large red building bearing the
initials MM. I drove through the factory gates, parked my
car and then asked to be taken to Mr. Morgan. I knew very
little about him at this time but assumed that he must, in
common with most factory owners, have a smart, luxurious
office with a big desk and comfortable chairs. I was therefore
surprised when I was taken through a long, dark shed filled
with every conceivable kind of Morgan spare part to a little
bare wooden door with no label. 'He's there,' said my guide.

I knocked and was told to come in, and entered what
must be regarded as the holy of holies of the Morgan world—
Peter Morgan's office. It was not quite the holy of holies I
had expected but I was immediately delighted. It was small,
and the cream paint on the walls had begun to turn yellow
with age. The walls were covered with photographs of
Morgans of all ages and covering the floorboards in the
centre part of the room was a small square of well-worn
carpet. In the midst of all this there was a simple unvarnished

table covered with papers, behind which sat Peter Morgan. I suddenly realized how foolish I had been to imagine anything different, for H.F.S.* had always been the most modest of men, even though he was extremely rich towards the end of his life. Anything that was good enough for H.F.S. was certainly good enough for Peter. Thus the Morgan office could not have been anything other than it was—nothing else could have truly matched either the personality of the Morgan family or of the car.

Mr. Morgan received me very kindly and we talked for some time about his cars. I felt afterwards that meeting him and getting to understand him made it much easier to understand the personality and eccentricity of his cars. He made it clear that Morgans had built fine sports cars in his father's time and that that was precisely what they would always do. He explained that he loved owning and running Morgan Motors because he was able to build exactly the car that he wanted to build, and that fortunately this coincided with the taste of the Morgan-owning public.

My interview over, I collected the spare parts I had come for and set off for home feeling very much wiser. Three weeks or so then passed during which I took WXA 6 from the coachbuilder to the sprayer, from the sprayer to the upholsterer, and from the upholsterer to the local garage, until finally she was ready, looking in every way as fine as on the day she was born ten years earlier. I drove home where a ceremonial bottle of Malvern water was poured over the front of the car to mark the launching of her new lease of life. Then I took my family for their first ride. As I said before, I was not at this time fully aware of all the hazards of Morgan motoring, and I was just as surprised as my passengers when at about 40 m.p.h., with a lorry bearing down close behind us, the front wheels began to shimmy so violently that I had to stop at once. Later, I rang up Morgans' service department to ask what the trouble might be as the local garage could find nothing loose or defective.

'Oh, that is quite normal,' said Morgans. 'All you need to do is to put the inner edge of each front tyre on to the outer edge of its wheel every ten thousand miles. If you do that you will be quite all right.'

Although I did not say so at the time, I felt quite angry at being told such nonsense by Morgan engineers. Was the next step to tell me to put a ground-up toad's tongue in the

* The founder of Morgans: H. F. S. Morgan is always referred to simply as H.F.S.

The author's Morgan in the Quadrangle of Mansfield College, Oxford

sump? Nevertheless I tried out this idea and to my amazement I have never had a shimmy since. I now realize that there are many adjustments that have to be made to Morgans which are the mechanical counterparts of what in the medical world are called old wives' remedies.

It was not many weeks after this that the Oxford term began again and so the Morgan was loaded up with my things and I returned to my studies. The car had an instant impact in the university which it had never enjoyed while in its black and rusty condition. The first few days of that term were spent in an exhausting effort to postpone at least some of the demands for rides made by every member of the college. All sorts of curious people would stop and look at the car and sometimes come and see me about it (this was perfectly possible because by University regulations I was obliged to have a ticket on the window bearing my name and college). Perhaps the most interesting of my visitors was a monk who told me that the hardest decision of his life had been taken when he decided to give up his Morgan on entering his order. The other pleasures of the world he found

Oxford dons were often impressed by the Morgan—the man with both arms in the air is a lecturer in Medieval English

easy to dispense with, but to give up the Morgan was asking a lot. All monks go through a ceremony in which a monastic robe and a sports coat are laid side by side on a table and the aspiring monk has to take the robe in preference to the sports coat. My friend had asked if a model of a Morgan could be substituted for the sports coat, but after much thought in important ecclesiastical circles his request was turned down. After my meeting with Brother Richard, a Positano-yellow Morgan containing three monks in their robes and one layman in a deerstalker was regularly to be seen in the streets of Oxford.

It was, of course, above all in the Summer Term that the Morgan really came into its own. The joys of the Oxford Summer Term are always plentiful, but the joys of a Morgan Summer Term are even greater. The car made every journey a great event and whether it was going down to the Cherwell Boathouse to hire a punt or out to Horton-cum-Studley for tea, it was always fun. A beautiful girl in the passenger seat was all that was needed to make life quite idyllic and the Morgan made this commodity easy to come by. Eccentric dons were also usually very struck by the car and some of them used the opportunity of driving in it to shout quotations from medieval literature at passers-by.

The knowledge that three years' worth of work is to be examined at the end of one's last Summer Term is enough to frighten the calmest of students, and I realized that if I attempted to do my revision in stuffy libraries, I would get nowhere. I therefore arranged a very agreeable programme which enabled me to get through an enormous volume of work without growing stale. I would set off after breakfast armed with books, pipe and sandwiches and drive out of town until I found a quiet lane in which I could park. There I would move into the back seat of the car which became my study and library. It was certainly fortunate that the summer proved to be an exceptionally good one for I was able to work in this way throughout the term.

I could fill a whole volume with descriptions of people's reactions to the Morgan, both at home and abroad, but I must refrain from that pleasure. I can only sum up by saying that when it is snowing and the snow drifts in, there are times when I wish that the weather protection were better. When I go fast down a bumpy lane, there are times when I wish the suspension were softer. Yet there is nothing that I would really like to change, for it is a car that gives so much pleasure just as it is. An enthusiast once remarked to Mr. Morgan, 'I get such a kick out of Morgans that I regard their use as transport as purely incidental; in fact as a kind of bonus.' I am inclined to agree.

Finally, I ought perhaps to say just a word about how this book came to be written: I have, since the age of about seven, been continually frustrated by the fact that no complete history of Morgans has been available. In order to put an end to this frustration I thought I had better try to write one myself. I therefore made contact with Peter Morgan some months before taking my history degree and asked him if he approved of my plan. He said he did and so, apart from a brief flirtation with the business world, I have spent my time since leaving university working on this book. I need hardly say that to spend one's days immersed in the Morgan family albums and wandering about Malvern is little short of bliss to the Morgan enthusiast. I hope that through this book I may be able to pass on to others some of the pleasure I have had in writing it.

The Early History 1884·1914

Throughout the latter part of the nineteenth century and the early decades of the twentieth, the souls of the people of Stoke Lacey in Herefordshire were in the care of a remarkable family—the Morgans. Thus when Harry Morgan ('H.F.S.' to the *cognoscenti*) was born in 1884, his birthplace was the Old Rectory at Stoke Lacey. His grandfather had been vicar for sixteen years and his father, George Morgan, was at that time almost eight years into his sixty-year reign as curate and vicar. In spite of being born into such an ecclesiastical family, there was never any great likelihood of H.F.S. following in his father's footsteps, both because George Morgan was a remarkably broadminded man and because his son began to display a talent for things mechanical at an early age.

H.F.S. was educated at Marlborough and his sister, Dorothy, recalls that quite soon after he went there (in 1897) he was summoned to appear before the headmaster, who said: 'It is all very well for you to have inventive genius but it is an intolerable nuisance at school.' This comment came as a result of some of H.F.S.'s scientific experiments which had nearly ended in disaster. Unfortunately his time at Marlborough was destined to be brief: in common with most of the public schools at that time the food there was appalling and it was not long before undernourishment began to have a detrimental effect on his health. On one occasion when the boys were given ham with such a large content of maggots that it could be seen rocking gently on

George Morgan with his daughter, Dorothy, in 1913

the plates, H.F.S. was delegated by his friends to complain
to the housemaster. Inevitably, he received a very severe
reprimand while the food continued to be as bad as ever.
Eventually his parents decided to withdraw him from
Marlborough and there was for a short time a possibility
that he might go to an art school. George Morgan was an
amateur artist and would probably have been quite pleased
if his son had taken up the subject; yet he made it absolutely
clear that H.F.S. was free to choose for himself between art
and engineering.

Dorothy Morgan says that her parents took Harry to
Italy at this time to try to encourage his interest in art, but
it seems more likely that the trip was arranged so as to help
restore his health after leaving school. Although George
Morgan remained fond of painting all his life, and after the
death of his wife spent much of his free time with his easel,
his son was more inclined towards engineering and so went
to Crystal Palace Engineering College.

H.F.S. quickly showed that the ingenuity he had displayed
at Marlborough was a sign of things to come, for he was an

H.F.S. the founder, in 1913

immediate success. He loved his time at the college and the more opportunity he had to design and build things, the more his abilities came to the fore. Perhaps his most famous achievement at the college was that of comfortably breaking the bicycling speed record on a machine designed and built by himself—this was a foretaste of what he was destined to spend his life doing in cars. By the time that he left Crystal Palace, no one could doubt that he was a competent draughtsman and designer.

It was remarkable that his father should have supported and encouraged H.F.S.'s career in engineering at a time when people still thought very badly of clergymen's sons going into trade, and it seems that his reason for doing so was simply that he was a great family man. He was devoted to his children and always put their interests far above what other people might say. Added to this, he was a great enthusiast and loved to share exciting ideas and projects with his children. Thus he again helped his son by arranging for him to be taken under the wing of William Dean, chief engineer of the Great Western Railway works at Swindon, when he left Crystal Palace. Men like William Dean were in the habit of taking on one or two pupils rather as the great Harley Street surgeons take on one or two housemen. It provided them with a little extra income and gave them an opportunity to pass on their talents, but since there were always more eager pupils than there were places for them, George Morgan did well to arrange this for his son.

Under William Dean's care, H.F.S. received an extremely comprehensive engineering training and had a chance to observe and work in every shop at the works. The value of the training is perhaps proved by the fact that one of the pupils at another railway works at this time was W. O. Bentley. Peter Morgan often wonders whether their respective training places influenced H.F.S. to build small cars and W. O. Bentley to build large ones.

H.F.S. was so successful at Swindon that when his training period came to an end, the Great Western Railway eagerly asked him to stay on permanently. But he had never wanted a career in railways—he had always seen the training at Swindon as a means to more adventurous things. So he left the railway in 1906 and opened a garage at Malvern Link, with agencies for Darracq and Wolseley.

When the garage was established and going well, H.F.S. began to think of launching a new venture. He therefore bought a 10-h.p. Wolseley bus and began to operate a service between Malvern and Worcester. He hoped that people would be glad to have swift and easy transport available, but in this he was wrong: Malvern was then, as it is to some extent still, a town full of retired colonels and other peace-loving people. They hated the innovation of a bus service and were shocked that a clergyman's son should be involved in such an enterprise. Letters began to pour into his garage complaining about every aspect of the bus service. H.F.S. was shrewd enough to deal with this. He put many of the letters on display in his window so that the townspeople could have a good laugh at them, and this swiftly put a stop to the flow of correspondence. Nevertheless, the bus service was not a success; the people of Malvern seemed far more interested in boycotting it than in supporting it, and so H.F.S. sold his bus and, together with a partner called Leslie Bacon, entered the hire-car business. It was characteristic of his modesty that if ever a customer offered him a tip, he was

Mr. Stephenson-Peach in the car H.F.S. built in the Malvern College workshops in 1909

happy to accept it, whereas Mr. Bacon made it clear that it was beneath his dignity to do so.

During this time, H.F.S. remained an enthusiastic cyclist, and in spite of owning a garage often chose to cycle over to Stoke Lacey. In 1908, however, he became interested in the idea of building himself a motor-cycle and with this in view bought a twin-cylinder 7-h.p. Peugeot engine. However, he then decided that while he enjoyed cycling, he could not feel the same about motor-cycling. This turned his thoughts towards building some sort of cyclecar. It used to be said that the financial set-back caused by crashing a hired Benz on a hill near Hereford obliged him to build rather than buy a car for himself, but this seems very doubtful! In the first place, the crash repairs only came to £28, and secondly, being in the car trade, H.F.S. could have used one of the cars in stock for his own transport without ever actually owning a car. Thus it must have been a more creative desire that prompted him to build his first three-wheeler.

He had two friends in Malvern who were always involved in ingenious pranks, such as making cars that had to be driven backwards: they were the Stephenson-Peach brothers whose father was the engineering master at Malvern College. It was with Mr. Stephenson-Peach's help that H.F.S. was able to build himself a car over a twelve-month period in the college workshops. The work began in 1908 and was completed early in 1909, and there can be no doubt that without the help of Malvern College's workshops the project would have been impossible. It was the only place within several miles that had the necessary equipment to carry out the complicated machining which the car required. As he was still fully involved in selling and hiring cars, H.F.S. could never have found the time to build the first Morgan if he had had to do this work far away from Malvern.

The car was constructed very lightly and was based on a tubular chassis held together by skilful brazing. The principal tube in the chassis ran from the front to the rear of the car. This tube had two transversely extending members at the front to which the Peugeot engine was fitted and on to which H.F.S.'s extremely advanced front suspension (almost identical to that used on the Plus-8 to this day) was mounted. The main drive shaft ran through this tube to the gearbox at the rear. Here two dog clutches and two short chains (one for each of the two speeds—no reverse) comprised the transmission system. Braking was by means of two bands mounted on either side of the rear wheel, one of which was attached to the footbrake and the other to the handbrake.

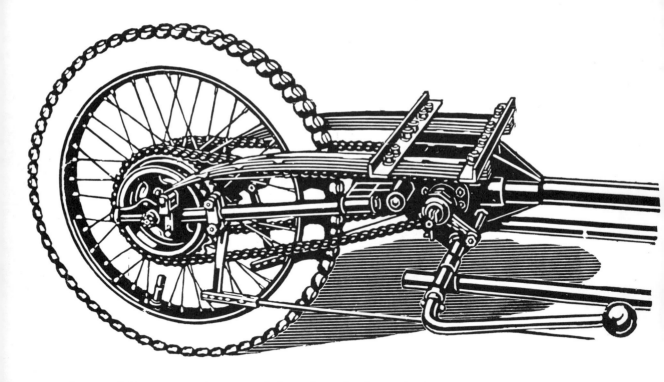

*Rear and front suspension as used throughout the three-wheeler period.
Modifications were made, but the general design remained the same*

Steering was by means of a tiller which could conveniently be controlled from the single seat, and bodywork as such was almost non-existent, although the smart flat petrol tank at the front and the mudguards gave an illusion of it. H.F.S. must have been very keen on making the utmost use of tubes, for the two parallel longitudinal tubes which made up the rest of the chassis were used as silencer extensions.

When the three-wheeler finally emerged from the workshops, H.F.S.'s friends were at once impressed. It was one of the first British cars ever to have independent front suspension; the only other car in the world at that time with anything comparable was the French Sizaire-Naudin, and even this only had a transverse spring to each side rather than a fully independent pair of springs. The other great feature of the car was its remarkably high power-to-weight ratio of 90 b.h.p. per ton, which in effect immediately enabled the Morgan to be thought of as a sports car. Although H.F.S. had built his machine entirely in the spirit of a do-it-yourself hobby, it quickly attracted considerable outside attention. More and more of his friends began to ask him to build a similar car for them and to make his cars available to the public. It was this pressure from his friends and from other local people that first made H.F.S. think of the possibility of making cars as a business, and so he approached his father, George, who was delighted to support his son in this venture, as in all others. He provided the money to enable him to set up a workshop and buy the necessary equipment. The Morgan Motor Company was now launched.

But the launching of his car was not the only important event in H.F.S.'s life after leaving the G.W.R. workshops. As has been the case with so many men of creative ability, he received much moral support from his wife, and so it was an important evening in 1907 when he went to a dance at the Grand Hotel in Malvern, which has since become Malvern Girls' College. Here he met Ruth Day, daughter of the vicar of St. Matthias, Malvern Link. The hotel was very near the station and couples would often sit out between dances on benches along the platforms—not perhaps the most romantic of places but, nevertheless, it was there that the great romance of his life began. Ruth was a very active and capable girl, and after they were married she regularly joined him for trials and competitions of all sorts and encouraged him in his downhearted moments. In spite of her devotion to his work, she found time to have six children, five girls and one son—Peter.

There can be no doubt that the Morgans were a fine

family team, ideally suited to launching a business. George Morgan was a hearty extrovert enthusiast who was an excellent spokesman for the company, both verbally and by letter, and was blessed with a head for figures quite good enough to cope with the company's finances for several years. H.F.S. was a quieter, more dedicated engineer-enthusiast, and Ruth was a fine morale-booster. Such a trio was bound to meet with success and success did, of course, come—although not immediately.

The Morgan three-wheeler was first reviewed in *The Motor Cycle* in November 1910, just after it had appeared at the First International Cycle and Motor Cycle Exhibition at Olympia. The reviewer begins by saying that the car should on no account be missed by visitors, and concludes by describing it as 'a very cleverly designed runabout for a single rider'. Herein lay one of the two major reasons for the lack of immediate success—people who liked the car held back from buying it because they would not be able to take a passenger in it. The other reason for the somewhat slow launching of the car was the simple fact that it had not proved itself in trials and competitions, and this counted even more significantly in the early part of this century than it does now. Those who doubt this should read the letter signed 'Enthusiast' in *The Motor Cycle* of November 1912, in which the writer says: 'There are only three cyclecars the manufacturers of which have had the courage to compete in all or most of the yearly reliability trials, viz. the A.C., the Morgan and the G.W.K. I venture to suggest that until the manufacturers of other cyclecars publicly demonstrate their quality . . . intending purchasers and especially the businessman, will not look at the results of their time and labour.'

H.F.S. was not slow to tackle both these matters, and in the meantime he was helped by Harrods taking on the first agency. The great Knightsbridge store was still an up-and-coming firm at this time and did not fail to notice any product with an interesting potential. Thus they were in touch with Mr. Morgan soon after the show and made an agreement which benefited both sides. Other agencies soon followed.

Comfortably before the 1911 Motor Cycle Show, H.F.S. had his two-seater Runabout ready for display. A contemporary drawing had this caption: 'The Morgan Magnet attracts all young couples by its double seating accommodation.' Moreover, the previous year had given him a chance to prove his car, so that 1911 reviews were very enthusiastic. After the show, *Motor Cycling* commented: 'The interest

The first production Morgan two-seater, shown at the Motor Cycle Show in 1911

displayed in the Morgan Runabouts was phenomenal. As all our readers know, these machines have competed with unqualified success in all the big trials of the last 18 months gaining a reputation of which the makers may justly be proud.'

Another reviewer was quick to whet the appetites of many motor-cycle enthusiasts when he commented: 'The advent of so practical a vehicle will be of immense attraction to the motor-cyclist who wants to take a passenger and yet remain a motor-cyclist. . . . The Morgan is wonderfully stable, being quite low, has a top speed of 45 m.p.h. and has climbed every hill to which it has been put.'

Another reviewer struck enthusiasm for Morgans into the heart of every budding Casanova when he intimated that a special type of Morgan Matchmaker duo-car would shortly make its appearance, in which the seat would be made

The erecting shop and the machine shop in 1912

considerably less roomy than standard and the control actuated by pedals so that only one hand would need to be employed in driving.

Those who looked for comfort also enthused over the Morgan, and especially over its hand-starter which the driver could operate from his seat without getting out of the car. Thus the car attracted the widest possible range of potential customers: its high power-to-weight ratio made it ideal for sporting young men and gave Morgans the right to call themselves 'First of the Real Sports Cars'; the low price meant that it was within range of most people's pockets (the cheapest model costing only £65 at that time), and such luxurious features as the hand-starter meant that even brave young ladies could run a Morgan. All these factors, together with ruggedness, durability and reliability proven in trials, meant that by the end of 1911 H.F.S. had really succeeded, and in fact the successes were to continue in an uninterrupted stream.

From his own point of view, H.F.S. found trials and competitions quite worrying and those who knew him will say that he used to suffer slightly from nerves as the starting time approached. This was, of course, nothing to do with the fact that he might have an unpleasant accident or lose his personal reputation as a competent driver. It was simply that he believed very sincerely in the quality and potential of his cars but did not believe so fervently in his own ability to do them justice; and so, while he loved being involved in competitions, he could not look upon them with the same detachment as those whose business success could not be adversely affected by them.

H.F.S. need not have worried, for the Morgan successes up to the end of 1911 more than justified one of the early handbooks remarking in its introduction: 'The Morgan Runabout has been before the public for two years and during that time has proved its efficiency and reliability in all the most important public trials. It has a great advantage therefore over untried and unsuccessful machines.' Surely no new owner could fail to be impressed by such an introduction to his purchase.

1912 brought two striking successes for Morgans. On 27th March the first cyclecar race ever to be held at Brooklands was run. There were seven starters, and the winner was Harry Martin, the motor-cyclist of J.A.P. fame, who brought his Morgan home first at an average speed of 57 m.p.h.

Even more significant was H.F.S.'s spectacular feat in

covering just a few yards short of sixty miles in one hour, also at Brooklands, in November of that year. As *The Cyclecar* said: 'In the motoring world, the hour record is regarded as one of the severest tests to which it is possible to subject a machine, be it car, motor bicycle or cyclecar. Few machines survive this test and those which do may be regarded as absolutely reliable and sturdily constructed vehicles.'

Throughout 1912, attempts were being made to break the hour record and thus secure the Cyclecar Trophy for 1913. In May, a Bédélia covered $43\frac{1}{2}$ miles in one hour, only to be defeated one month later by a G.W.K. which covered 45 miles. But G.W.K. did not hold the record for long and in July Bédélia won it back again by covering almost $45\frac{1}{4}$ miles. In August another Bédélia driven by another driver added 226 yards on to the July record! But Bédélia was unable to sustain its lead, and in late August J. T. Wood covered 48 miles in his G.W.K.—a record that stood for six weeks. It was at this juncture that H.F.S. joined the fray and made the struggle to rise from $43\frac{1}{2}$ miles to 48 miles seem like a joke. At his first attempt he covered no less than 55 miles. Wood, who had felt comfortably ahead until this time, was much put out by this, and within a few days was back at Brooklands with a new record of almost 56 miles. It therefore became imperative that H.F.S. should prove that a Morgan could exceed 56 miles if he was to preserve his reputation and win the Cyclecar Trophy. Dorothy Morgan well remembers 23rd November 1912; she remembers how her brother felt on that morning—that his whole future depended on his performance that day. To a certain extent he was right; the Morgan Motor Company could not afford to lose the one-hour record. The trial began and from the start it was clear that all was going well; nevertheless the joy felt by the Morgan family and their supporters knew no bounds when they heard that H.F.S. had not only won back the record, but had also come within a few yards of achieving the almost magical mile per minute for one hour. George must have been sorely tempted to throw his top hat into the air with delight.

The prestige resulting from this success meant that future advertisements could carry this comment: 'The Morgan is the fastest cyclecar in existence and it proves by its wonderful performance at Brooklands that a three-wheeler not only holds the ground at any speed—but does so better than a four-wheeler.'

There was surely a ring of George Morgan in that remark,

Nº 2.

4TH DECEMBER, 1912.
ONE PENNY.
Registered at the G.P.O. as a News

The Cyclecar

"Nearly 60 miles in one hour"

The front cover of The Cyclecar, *4th December 1912, after H.F.S. covered nearly 60 miles in one hour (George Morgan in top hat)*

for the archives are full of letters written by him in defence of three wheels.

1913 was another successful year for Morgans and no success was greater than their victory at the French Cyclecar Grand Prix at Amiens in July. As early as April, *The Cyclecar* was full of comments about the forthcoming Grand Prix and was lamenting the small number of entries. This was especially feeble in view of the fact that belt-driven cyclecars could in almost all cases be modified for racing at small cost, by providing higher gears and a streamlined body. However, lack of enterprise was not the only reason for the limited entry: the regulations, which were full of petty restrictions, were also to blame. The definition of a cyclecar was too narrow and it seemed unreasonable to make the competitors insure for all risks, including setting fire to the grandstand! Indeed the Morgan entries were by no means certain to be accepted at all, as the French did not regard three-wheelers as cyclecars. In spite of the uncertainty, Violet-Bogey entered 3 cars, Bédélia 3, Mathis 1 four-cylinder machine, Ronteix 1 four-cylinder water-cooled machine, Noel 1 twin air-cooled car, du Guesclin 1 four-cylinder water-cooled car, Automobilette 2 cars and Super 1. In all, 38 cyclecars were entered.

The English entries included 2 G.N.s, 2 Duos, 1 Bolton-Precision, 1 Marlborough, 1 Sphinx-Globe and 4 Grand Prix Morgans. The Morgans were all fitted with water-cooled engines and were of less than 1,000 c.c. capacity to comply with the rules. The Morgans entered by H. F. S. Morgan and W. G. McMinnies both had $90 \times 77\frac{1}{2}$ m.m. overhead valve J.A.P. engines, while Mr. Holder used a Blumfield engine. The fourth car, driven by Mr. Mundy, had a Green-Precision engine. All four cars had chassis 11 in. longer than standard and this made it possible to lower the seats by transferring them from on top of the gearbox to either side of the propeller-shaft. The steering columns were very raked, and the petrol and oil filler caps were spring-held and of large diameter to facilitate speedy filling-up. The Morgans were fitted with double petrol pipes between the tank and the carburettor, so that a spare was available, and foot-controlled oil pumps in connection with Best and Lloyd's semi-automatic drip-feed system of lubrication were also planned.

Another important modification was the enlargement to $1\frac{1}{2}$ in. of the diameter of the two chassis tubes which carried the exhaust gases. The cars had 3-in. tyres on Voiturette rims and it was decided not to select the gear ratios until after the cars had arrived in France, so that they should be perfectly suited to the course. The total weight of each of these cars was, incidentally, only 3 cwt.

The Cyclecar was especially impressed by Mr. Mundy's Green-Precision engine: 'It is one of the finest productions we have ever seen . . . and an excellent feature and one specially produced for the Morgan machine is the enclosing of the magneto drive in an oil-and-dust-proof aluminium case which makes the whole machine appear neat and workmanlike.' Equally neat and workmanlike were the gauze screens fitted in front of the engines of all four Morgans to protect them from flying stones hurled up by the wheels of other machines.

By June 1913, excitement over the French Grand Prix was reaching fever-heat and *The Cyclecar* predicted that Amiens would be the scene of the most exciting and speedy racing ever seen. More significantly, that wise magazine proclaimed Morgans and Bédélias as the favourites for the race: 'On the French side of the channel they [Morgans] are looked upon as the most dangerous of the English competitors.'

Because of all the interest taken in the Grand Prix, many descriptions of the race were published, not the least of which is that of Mr. W. G. McMinnies who wrote for *The Cyclecar* and was himself a competitor.

'A few minutes before noon, all the machines entered in the cyclecar Grand-Prix were lined up on the specially-constructed track, with the grandstands on their left and the row of tyre and petrol pits immediately on their right. The starts were given in groups of three, the road being sufficiently wide for this. This arrangement provided a most interesting spectacle for it gave the riders an opportunity of showing their skill in getting away from a standing start. The first three were sidecar machines, one of which was so slow in getting off from the start that Mr. McMinnies in the second group was quickly after it and passed it in the outer bend leading into the first leg of the course. The Morgan was remarkably quick in getting away—its liveliness and stability calling for most favourable comment.

'Nos. 7 and 8 Morgans started at the same instant, the latter machine, driven by Mr. Mundy, getting the advantage as soon as the straight way was reached. Within only minutes of the last cars having set off, a bugle call sounded and McMinnies' car came into sight cornering very fast thanks to the low build and wide track of his Morgan. A minute later another Morgan driven by Mundy appeared. He took the first corner wide at about 35 m.p.h. and the offside front wheel was seen practically to double up under the strain. At the second bend it was on the point of collapsing, so Mundy had to pull up and abandon the race. This was very sad as he had achieved the third fastest lap and the Green-Precision V-type engine was going beautifully. After a few more minutes, consternation became very great over the non-appearance of H. F. S. Morgan's Morgan. Subsequently it was learned that a con-rod had broken 3 miles out from the start, probably because of the high compression ratio, and this had put H.F.S. out of the race.'

Mr. McMinnies said he began his race flying along at about 50 m.p.h. with the throttle just half-open. He could tell the speed was high because he could not understand at all what his passenger said, nor could his passenger hear what he said to him. His first problem came when a plug began to misfire. The trouble quickly became worse and soon he had to stop to change the plugs. Thanks to a special spanner that had been made to extract the right-hand plug, this tricky job was quickly achieved and he set off again. At this stage McMinnies was in the lead by position, although not by time. But the lead did not last long, for after the second lap, when entering some of the double bends under the bridge at Bores, he found he could not control the steering and looking down after a few hundred yards, discovered that a front tyre was flat. The cause of the puncture was in fact a broken piece of valve-spring that had worked its way into the tyre and it took McMinnies and his partner twelve minutes to replace the tube. When he got under way again, he was never passed by another machine.

McMinnies described his most exciting moment as follows: 'He passed one of the long rakish-looking Bédélias on the narrow, winding cross-roads, which connect the two lips of the triangle. He was doing nearly fifty and had to drive on the grass to get past, although the Frenchman sportingly gave him as much room as he could.'

McMinnies' colleagues were able to communicate after another lap or so that he was lying fifth. He therefore decided to put on a little more speed, but never to force the engine more than was necessary and never to take any risks on corners or bumps for fear of rattling the machine to pieces.

After completing five or six laps, McMinnies became horribly bored with the race and doubted whether he could complete the course. But as the speed increased, the laps seemed to decrease in length. He never had any sense of excitement or trepidation; every corner was negotiated with a comfortable margin of safety and even when passing other vehicles he never felt the slightest degree of alarm. By the time the tenth lap had been completed, McMinnies was lying third, the leader being Bonville in the Bédélia followed by Violet in the Violet-Bogey. Then, with great drama, in the eleventh lap Bonville's Bédélia caught fire and his passenger was slightly burned in stemming the flames. This cost him some time so that, by the beginning of the twelfth lap, Violet was in the lead (3 hrs. 2 mins. 50 secs.), McMinnies was second (3 hrs. 9 mins. 23 secs.), and Bourbeau in another Bédélia was third (3 hrs. 10 mins. 48 secs.). The latter had been fifth in the eighth lap and fourth in the tenth.

Although he realized that every second counted, McMinnies did not risk running out of petrol and stopped for a fill just before the beginning of the final lap. He also used the opportunity to secure a broken tie-rod. Such was the excitement felt by the Violet-Bogey supporters that they overdid their signalling and M. Violet in fact stopped and lost nearly a minute, costing him one place.

When McMinnies finished he had no idea that he had won and some time elapsed before he could be definitely

W. G. McMinnies and his mechanic Frank Thomas, after winning the French Cyclecar Grand Prix, 1913

placed first in both the sidecar and cyclecar class. It was a great triumph, and a French newspaper was amused to note that the very first thing McMinnies did at the end of the race was to light his pipe. His final comment was: 'It was a great race but I wish that the machine was twice as fast and that there were three times as many competitors to add to the excitement; but in the meantime, *Vive* Morgan and *Vivra* the cyclecar.'

His average speed was 41.9 m.p.h. for the 162.9 miles of the race, and he attributed his success almost completely to the great thoroughness with which his mechanic, Frank Thomas, had prepared the car (he was also his companion in the race). Every nut and bolt on the whole machine was spring-washered, taped and shellacked, and in many cases, split pins were used in addition. A trouble-free run was obviously the only thing to aim for and it was to the attention given to minute details that he owed his success. Tuning-up operations on the car had in fact begun three weeks previously in England. The final result of the Grand Prix was:

First	McMinnies	Morgan	3 hrs. 53 mins. 9 secs.
Second	Bourbeau	Bédélia	3 hrs. 55 mins. 54 secs.
Third	Violet	Violet-Bogey	3 hrs. 56 mins. 2 secs.

The victory was a very great triumph and a wonderful prestige-winner for Morgan. The *Cycle and Motorcycle Trader* said: 'It was a near thing but the Old Country did it; I said the Morgan was hot stuff.'

The *Scots Pictorial* sounded a patriotic note: 'The result of the racing was to demonstrate once more that British manufacturers have nothing to fear from foreign competition in any form of engineering or mechanical control and it is to be hoped that the lesson will not be lost upon that section of the trade who have set themselves resolutely against contests of all types.'

The *Pall Mall Gazette* commented: 'No one who is not on the inside of the racing game as it is played in France can realize the magnitude of the undertaking when a foreign competitor sets out to beat the French cracks at their own game—not that they do not play fairly, but they start with a heavy handicap in their favour for they are used to driving at high speeds on their own roads. They practically drive at racing speeds all the time they are on open highways and their corner-work is a thing to be admired.'

Next to the Amiens Grand Prix, the A.C.U. Six-Day

MORGAN

(Driven by Mr. W. G. McMinnies)

WINS the GRAND PRIX
Cyclecar and Sidecar Race.

For particulars and
list of Agents apply—

Price - from 85 Gns.

MORGAN MOTOR CO., LTD., MALVERN.

KINDLY MENTION "THE CYCLECAR" WHEN CORRESPONDING WITH ADVERTISERS.

Advertisement in The Cyclecar, *celebrating the Morgan victory at Amiens*

Trial was probably Morgan's greatest achievement in 1913. *The Cyclecar* headed its description of the trial 'A farcical test to destruction', and on the first day, half the cyclecar competitors had to retire. There were twelve cyclecar entrants including Singer, J.B.S., G.W.K., Morgan, Humberette, Chater Lea, Summers and Harding, Bédélia and Paragon. A machine called a Wall Tricarrier should have competed but it broke down early in the morning on the first day. There were two Morgans—one driven by H.F.S. and the other by Mr. Blackburn. H.F.S. had trouble with sooted plugs and to add to his difficulties was at one point almost completely out of oil, when a sporting motor-cycle competitor called Mr. Davis in a Clyno combination helped out with a spare can. When the competitors reached Ulldale Hill, which was a steep, unexpected ascent with a quarry-like surface, Mr. Chater Lea found that his machine seized up after the climb and the same fate befell Mr. Cooper's Humberette. As a result of the day's run there remained of the dozen entrants only two G.W.K.s, two Morgans, the Summers and Harding and the J.B.S.

'The competitors considered that the first day's route was extremely difficult but it was child's play to the second day.' Nevertheless, the second day only brought about one further retirement—that of Mr. Tamplin's G.W.K. The worst section was the five-mile climb through Sedbergh and Dent over an unmade track to Ingleton. The local inhabitants wagered that not a single machine would be able to climb this notorious by-lane which concludes with a 1-in-4 hairpin bend and has a surface resembling a river bed. Here Mr. Blackburn's Morgan came to a standstill and like the Summers and Harding had to be pushed up, but H.F.S. with his four gears was able to press on. (The J.B.S. also had to be assisted.)

The worst hazard in the afternoon was a deep and wide water-splash. H.F.S. took this rather fast, which resulted in his breaking an inlet valve. Both Morgans stopped but the delay caused was not disastrous. At the end of the day, one of the Morgans came in with a punctured tyre while the other had a broken bolt holding the rear coiled buffer-spring. The Summers and Harding was suffering from slipping belts and only the J.B.S. was in relatively sound condition.

One of the major hazards on the third day was the blinding dust encountered in the Lake District, especially in the region of Ulverston. As a result of strong protests from all the drivers, the average speed had been reduced for all the passenger machines over certain sections.

The major point of interest of the day was the reliability trial held ten miles out from Carlisle. This was on a fairly steep and straight incline, the first 50 yards being 1 in 12 and the next 200 yards 1 in 8. The competitors had to climb the first section at a speed between 7.2 and 5 m.p.h. and the second section between 18 and 20 m.p.h. All the cars fared quite well on this but later on there was a slight disaster when, as a result of being misdirected, H.F.S. went off on a half-hour detour. Nevertheless, by very skilful driving he managed to make up the time. But the third day ended sadly for Morgans when Blackburn broke his piston and cylinder. That left only Keiller's G.W.K., Morgan's Morgan and the J.B.S.

The fourth day was the most straightforward and there was very little drama or excitement at any stage.

On the fifth day, the J.B.S. for some reason started an hour late, but as it was a genuine mistake the driver was not penalized. Morgan had to change his rear tyre which cost him 22 minutes—a good time for the job. The morning was taken up by the Speed Trials which were held in conditions of driving rain and a blowing gale. After lunch, the weather was better and this was fortunate as the route lay through grass-grown lanes and bridle-paths, the worst of all being Kirkstone Pass in which the first mile averaged 1 in 6 and the last one-third mile had a gradient of 1 in 4. All three machines went well.

In the final result the best performance was put up by C. M. Keiller in his G.W.K. He won a gold medal and the special prize for the best performance in a four-wheel cyclecar. As the Morgan was officially classed as a sidecar, it had to compete with a sidecar combination to which it lost the passenger prize. Nevertheless, the Morgan won a gold medal and the J.B.S. only a bronze—it had lost marks for deviation in non-stop schedules and also for defective condition. The commentator in *The Cyclecar* said: 'The Morgan deserved special credit for winning the First Honours as the course was extremely trying for a three-tracker.'

Much publicity was given to the extreme difficulty of the trial and so the winning of a gold medal was very significant for Morgans. One of the very few voices that piped up in defence of the severity of the trial belonged to George Morgan, who said in a published letter: 'The Six-Day Trial is not intended to show which machines are sufficiently reliable for ordinary use any more than the Grand Prix is to point out which machines can reach the legal limit, but to show which are the most reliable. For this purpose the "test to destruction" is certainly more satisfactory than the absurdity of split seconds.'

The next outstanding Morgan success in 1913 came at the September speed trial at Brighton. There was a big entry and in some cases the same drivers were allowed to enter a large number of events. In each class there were two complete races; one for 'experts' under the A.C.U. classification and the other for 'generals'. An expert could enter for both races and a general for one. H.F.S. should have entered the race but unfortunately he was unable to start because he had smashed a big end during the week before the trial. This was probably caused by the much greater strain imposed on the working parts of the engine through the adoption of new steel pistons. Of the other Morgans, W. G. McMinnies drove the Grand Prix machine with which he had won at Amiens in August; W. South drove a G.P. Morgan; and Olliver's Morgan was fitted with a new type of radiator situated behind the J.A.P. side-by-side valve engine.

The result was an overwhelming victory for Morgans. In fact, the Morgan successes of 1913 were so impressive that the entire anticipated production for 1914 was completely booked up by the end of the Motor Cycle Show.

The 1913 Motor Cycle Show saw the introduction of no new models except for the specially modified Grand Prix models developed for Amiens. However, the Show served

Cars waiting to be despatched from the factory in 1913

to quash rumours that Morgans were going to bring out a four-wheeler cyclecar—although the correspondence of George Morgan in the motoring press should have made this obvious.

1913 ended with the London to Exeter trial in which A. B. T. Bashall and H. F. S. Morgan won gold medals It was held on Boxing Day 1913 and enabled Morgans to advertise themselves as the only car to have won gold medals every year since 1910. Twenty-one gold and seventeen silver medals were awarded to cars in the trial but it was very satisfactory that Morgan and Bashall should have done so well. A third Morgan driven by A. Mariani had to retire. The 1913 Exeter run brought the Morgan score for this event to ten gold medals in four years.

1914 did not get off to quite such a good start because of foul play by saboteurs at the Birmingham Cyclecar Trial, held in January. 'Some mischievous youngsters, suffragettes or enemies of the club, wilfully turned the direction signs with the result that drivers got on the wrong track.' Being a secret course, no competitor knew the route in advance and so the whole event was a shambles. One has to remember that these were days when there were people bitterly opposed to motoring and this sort of trouble was not un-common in some areas. When the trial was held again at the end of January, Morgans did rather well, V. Busby and R. D. Olliver both winning gold medals for their perfect scores. The club was obviously taking no chances over security: the R.A.C., the A.A. and the Boy Scouts were all called in to make sure that the route would be clear to drivers.

At the end of February the Cyclecar Club organized a General Efficiency Trial in which competitors sought to win the Westall Cup. The trial was widely publicized and was of considerable prestige value as cars had to show that they could respond extremely well to all sorts of different situations.

The Morgan entrants showed that they were quite equal to the tests that had been devised for them, and in a field of 32 starters H.F.S. came second, Busby tenth and Spencer twelfth. H.F.S.'s car looked like an air-cooled Standard model but, in fact, there was a J.A.P. water-cooled engine under the bonnet and the car was in effect equipped with four gears. I say in effect because it did not have a four-speed gearbox. Instead it had a two-speed gearbox behind the engine in addition to the ordinary Morgan dog-clutch mechanism which itself gave a choice of two speeds. The summary of the event given in *The Sportsman* was very flattering to Morgan: 'The results showed in a very pronounced manner the superiority of the light car as compared with the cyclecar. The Morgan driven by Mr. H. F. S. Morgan was the only conspicuously successful of the real cyclecars for this little three-wheeler would have been placed first instead of second except for hard luck at Brooklands.'

The late spring and early summer saw a number of gold medal wins for Morgan. Perhaps the most interesting event was the Cyclecar Club's Climb at Aston Hill in April. This was unusual in that it was a relay hill-climbing competition and it proved very successful. Two teams could enter at a time, each team having one car at the foot of the hill, one higher up and one still higher up. On being given the word to start, each of the two first competitors raced to his team-mate stationed higher, detached one sparking-plug, handed it to the other who inserted it in his engine, raced to the next competitor and repeated the process. No spanners could be handed from one competitor to another, but most wore gloves and so were able to escape the worst of the heat. Even so, several burned fingers resulted. The winning team included W. G. McMinnies and H. F. S. Morgan.

The last few months leading up to the outbreak of the First World War saw some remarkable Morgan successes abroad. Unfortunately I cannot name the journals from which the following quotes came, as my source has been a succession of untitled cuttings in the Morgan archives for 1914. One paper reported in May: 'The most consistent performer among the British cyclecars on the continent is the Morgan three-wheeler which has numerous successes to its credit in important competitions abroad. One of the latest Morgan successes was scored recently in a hill-climb near Marseilles where two of these machines were respectively first and second in the cyclecar class, their times beating those of 500-c.c. motor-cycles and of all touring cars except the specially designed racing machines.'

Another cutting describes the Paris–Rouen–Paris rally held at the beginning of June. 'Nine cars completed the Paris–Rouen-and-back course without loss of marks. The order of merit was decided by performances in the hill-climb. The order was: 1. Violet-Bogey (M. Violet) 2. Morgan (M. Black) 3. Automobilette.

'As usual the Morgan three-wheeler is maintaining its reputation—and incidentally that of the British Industry on the continent . . . the Paris–Rouen–Paris trial organised by the Touring Moto Club de France in which, of the nine light cars and cyclecars which finished without loss of marks, England was represented only by a Morgan. This machine was second in the hill-climb to M. Violet's Violet-Bogey but it defeated two other Violet-Bogeys with ease . . . a Violet-Bogey and a Morgan are entered for this year's G.P. and it will be interesting to see whether the Morgan repeats its last year's success when it defeated M. Violet's car by 2 mins. 53 secs.'

Finally, I think it is worth reproducing an article headed: 'The Morgan in the French Classics': 'In the three great autumn events in France the indefatigable Morgan three-wheeler will take part. In the G.P. a Morgan will be driven by Mr. Ware, in the international six days at Grenoble by H. F. S. Morgan and in the Circuit de Sarte by a French driver. Owing to many successes in French trials it is possible that the Morgan may be manufactured, for French sales only, in Paris; the demand in France making, we are informed, too great a demand on the Malvern works. The policy of H. F. S. Morgan in entering French events has thus been abundantly justified.'

But while all this activity was going on in France, the home front was not exactly quiet as is proved by an article in *The Cyclecar* of June 1914: 'On the 13 of June no fewer than fourteen Morgans were engaged in trials: five at Weston where they gained three firsts, one second and one

Typical hazard of cyclecar racing—Mr. Ellis's Morgan overturning in the A.C.U. Six-Day Trial of 1914 (H.F.S. often used a gauntleted hand to prevent himself tipping over)

third; two in the Cyclecar Club's half-day trial in which they gained non-stops; seven in the Motor Cycle Club's Inter-Club Trial. Of these only one was entered by the firm. This must nearly constitute a record.'

On 6th July the A.C.U. Six-Day Trial began. Despite all the rude comments that had been made against the A.C.U. in the previous year by competitors and motoring journalists, on account of the appalling difficulty of the course and the excessive speed, it was once again, to quote *The Cyclecar*, 'A Perfect Farce'. The heading in that journal said: 'The A.C.U. tests cyclecars to destruction over a course composed of grass-grown tracks and river-bed surfaces.' This was perhaps the only occasion in his competition experience on which H. F. S. Morgan was so disgusted by the organization of an event that he simply drove home when his number was called on the morning of the fourth day. Many cars turned over and an immense number of tyres were consumed. Nevertheless, W. G. McMinnies managed to complete the course in his Morgan (known as the Jabberwock) and W. James was also successful in his Morgan.

Some of the tests, such as one which required a speed of under 5 m.p.h. over the first 50 yards of a 1-in-7 hill, to be followed by 200 yards at 25 m.p.h., were so stiff that no one could do them. McMinnies came the closest to success, achieving almost 24 m.p.h. over the fast section. Considering the immense difficulty of the course the double Morgan success was a fine achievement.

July brought one further major success when E. B. Ware broke some records at Brooklands. Using his 750-c.c. Morgan, he beat the existing records for the flying kilometre and flying mile in the 750-c.c. class. His speed for the flying kilometre was 65.10 m.p.h. (previous record 61.12 m.p.h.), and the flying mile 63.09 (previous record 59.01 m.p.h.).

Towards the end of July, H.F.S. and his wife went over to France in preparation for the Six-Day International Trial which was due to begin at Grenoble early in August. Soon after landing in France he developed engine trouble and decided that it would be better to return to England rather than risk competing with an unsound engine. As it turned out, he left France on the day before the French Army was mobilized for the Great War. The trouble was therefore a blessing in disguise as it enabled him and his wife to return to England without having too worrying a time.

The mobilization of the French Army and the war clouds

on the horizon meant that all the exciting French competitions lined up for the late summer and the autumn had to be cancelled, and English drivers had to scuttle home before the guns opened fire.

But it took more than just a World War to prevent Morgans from building cars, as we shall see in the next chapter.

The Great Years of the Three-Wheeler 1914-1935

In spite of the outbreak of war, Morgan had some new models to offer towards the end of 1914. *The Motor Cycle* announced the new racing Morgan early in October: this had been specially developed for the Isle of Man International Cyclecar Race which was now postponed indefinitely. *The Cyclecar* of 12th October quoted 'a well-known man whose experience had been principally confined to high-power cars' as saying of the new Morgan: 'I've never

H.F.S. in the M.A.G.-engined Morgan racer developed for the 1914 Isle of Man International Cyclecar Race

been on anything like it since Lee Guiness took me up ——— hill at 88 m.p.h.'

This Morgan had an M.A.G. engine capable of developing nearly 30 b.h.p. Its top speed was 72 m.p.h., although with a streamlined, single-seat body even 80 m.p.h. might have been possible. The engine had eight valves (2 inlet and 2 exhaust to each cylinder) and in spite of its high compression, it was capable of turning over at slow speeds without knocking. The chassis was a modified version of the 1913 Grand Prix chassis but was longer in order to carry the seats even lower, and the rear brakes were increased in diameter. The car was described by *The Cyclecar* as being exceptionally good at cornering, and during a test at Brooklands it impressed its drivers by the way that, even when driven slowly, it bounced less than the Standard model, due to the fact that the rear coil springs had been dispensed with.

Although the war did not prevent Morgans from producing cars and bringing out new models, it did take its toll of competitions and these virtually ceased except for short-distance and unimportant trials. To make up for the absence of competition news the motoring journals filled up their pages with suggestions for all sorts of improvements that owners could make to their cars, such as chain guards and child seating accommodation, and also reported in detail controversies within the cyclecar movement. An American journal gave much food for thought when it suggested that the cyclecar was probably dead by late 1914. This produced some strong words, especially from George Morgan. In *The Cyclecar* of 2nd November 1914, he said: 'It is of course ridiculous to say that the cyclecar is dead; the output of Morgan, which is a cyclecar pure and simple, for the first six months of this year was double the output for the corresponding period in 1913 and nearly four times as large as in 1912. Surely, at a time when economy is becoming vastly important it is a mistake to throw cold water on a movement which especially aims at economy.'

Another favourite topic of the time was the cyclecar doing war work. An article mentioned Mr. Geoffrey Day, fellow and tutor of Emmanuel College, Cambridge, who had been H.F.S.'s passenger in the 1913 Grand Prix. He was photographed in uniform driving his Morgan. Another photograph showed a French dispatch-rider, Private Bloch, who had been a famous competition driver before the war, using his Morgan to deliver dispatches. And an article headed 'Lady Drivers and the Wounded' showed Mrs George W. Powell 'who drives her Morgan day and night on the

War work—Mrs George Powell in her Morgan, August 1915

St. John Ambulance Brigade duty in connection with the
feeding of the sick and wounded soldiers passing through
Snow Hill Rest Station, Birmingham'.

Morgans had been coming up to the thousand-car-per-
year mark before the war. Now, with their machine-shop
largely engaged in war work, this number was inevitably
reduced, but the flow of cars never stopped.

Such competitions as there were, before very tight petrol
rationing made them altogether impossible, were conducted
under conditions of considerable difficulty. The River Run
of the Cyclecar Club on 18th July 1915 had to be split up
into two detachments, owing to the transfer of a large number
of troops. It was impossible for the two groups to get together
for, after being pushed and ordered about, one half got into
Cookham and the other half ended up at Bisham Woods
near Marlow. It was sometimes necessary for competitors on
this run to wait for ten minutes with their engines running
while 'sundry battery mules and horses made up their minds
as to which side of the road they wanted'.

The spring of 1916 saw the advent of a new Grand Prix
Morgan with a far more streamlined and handsome body

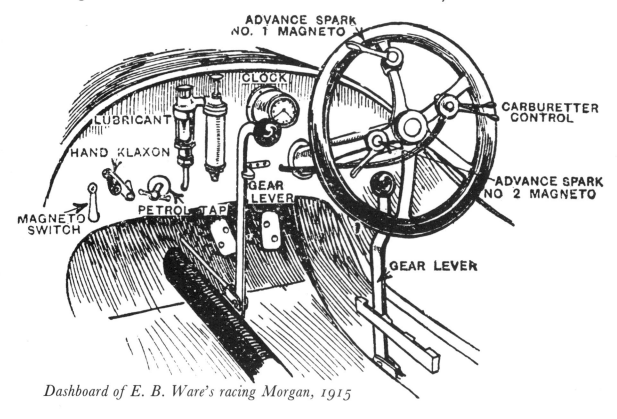

Dashboard of E. B. Ware's racing Morgan, 1915

than the 1915 racer. It had a 10-h.p. M.A.G. engine and a lengthened chassis, as this was found to give greater stability and better road-holding. Otherwise there were no major alterations to the previous model. But there could be no question of this car's being available in any sizeable quantities, for on 15th November 1916 the Minister of Munitions issued an order prohibiting the manufacture of motor cars without a permit. George Morgan protested violently that the suddenness with which this order was issued would cause severe difficulties for firms with a stock of parts or of partly built cars; but it was to no avail. In fact the Morgan Motor Company was not too badly hit by this as its investment of £20,000 in the War Loan showed. Besides, permits were quite readily issued to build cars for sale abroad and accordingly Morgans were exported from Malvern during the war to France, Russia, Canada, Bolivia and India. Even if Morgans had been allowed to continue producing cars for the home market they would not have sold many: the petrol situation became acute early in 1917 and the Petrol Committee stopped the issue of petrol licences to all except those 'engaged on work of national importance for which the continued use of a motor car or motor cycle is essential'.

Perhaps the only event of any importance to Morgans in 1917 was the purchase of a specially modified Grand Prix model, by the man who was almost certainly the greatest air ace of the war: Captain Albert Ball, V.C., who had shot down more than forty German aeroplanes by the time he was himself shot down—about one month after taking delivery of his car.

Captain Albert Ball, V.C., with his M.A.G.-engined Grand Prix Morgan, 1917

Mr. C. Potter's gas-propelled Morgan, 1918

On the technical side probably the greatest development of 1918 was the advent of the gas-fuelled Morgan. Two gentlemen called Edwards and Parry, who ran a garage in Great Portland Street, constructed a frame above their Morgan which supported a large gas bag measuring 7 ft. 10 in. long, 4 ft. wide, and 3 ft. high. This bag held enough gas for 30 miles of driving and the contents cost about one shilling. It took about ten minutes to fill it with gas. A half-inch flexible gas pipe connected the bag to the Amac carburettor and no alteration to this was found necessary. The flow of gas was simply controlled: first of all by a handcock and secondly by a butterfly valve connected to the accelerator pedal. The whole set-up worked extremely effectively and there was no difficulty in starting. Another gentleman experimenting with this type of conversion at the same time was a Mr. C. Potter of Leeds, but he had found it necessary to modify the carburation by adding the spraying chamber of a B. & B. carburettor to the air intake of his Amac carburettor.

At long last, on 11th November 1918, the Armistice was signed and the First World War ended. Morgans wasted no time in getting back into action and their advertisement in *The Cyclecar* of 25th November 1918 was headed 'An Early Return to Something like the "Good Old Times".' It went on to point out that as from 1st December holders of stocks of petrol or petrol licences could use their Morgans for any purpose within 30 miles of their homes, and that in January petrol would become available to anyone who had or could obtain a car. People were therefore urged to put their names on the Morgan waiting list at once, and many hastened to do so.

By early 1919 car production had returned to the fifteen-car-per-week mark in spite of hold-ups caused by outside suppliers of parts. Already the first bays of the new Pickersleigh Road factory were in use as a body-finishing shop and only one incident clouded the very rosy picture for Morgans at this time: while passing a capstan lathe in the turning-shop H.F.S. slipped on a small patch of grease. To save himself he threw out his right hand which caught in the machine, with the result that the first two fingers of this hand had to be amputated.

Despite the difficulty of obtaining supplies, many of the 1919 Morgans were fitted with 8-h.p. J.A.P. engines,* and the return of petrol soon brought about the return of competitions and trials. Morgans were not slow to return to the limelight and in the London–Edinburgh trial held in June 1919 they were awarded four gold medals and one silver. Four of the five Morgans entered succeeded in reaching Edinburgh from London within twenty-three hours. More honours followed in July when F. J. Findon, the senior assistant editor of *The Light Car*, made the fastest climb in a standard machine at the South Harting hill-climb, and then in the Midland Cycle and Athletic Club's 200-mile trial (which involved covering eighty miles before breakfast), Mr. H. Denley's Morgan swept the board, carrying off all the major prizes.

September 1919 brought the first post-war A.C.U. Six-Day Trial. For the first time it seemed that some of the rude

* Possibly the supply position was helped by the fact that Mr. E. B. Ware, head of J.A.P. Experimental Department, was a great Morgan enthusiast!

The erecting shop and the despatch bay in the new factory, 1919

comments made before the war about the absurd difficulty of the event had been heeded, for 110 of the 111 starters on the first day survived the test. Seven Morgans were entered, their drivers being H. F. S. Morgan, E. W. Merrall, F. W. James, H. Greaves, W. D. Hawkes, S. Hale and N. Svanso. One of the new features in the trial was a noise-level test, in which up to 10 out of the total of 200 marks could be awarded for silent running. The test was carried out on an audiometer, a very large piece of electronic equipment, which had been invented by Maj. A. M. Low. He also operated it for the test.

Unfortunately, on the second day Hawkes had to retire with timing trouble and Greaves had a narrow escape when water was accidentally put into his petrol tank at a refilling point! The whole tank was immediately drained and fortunately no trouble resulted. Of the 111 starters, 81 finished, and Morgans won one gold, two silver and one bronze medal. The gold was won by H.F.S. and enabled the company to continue the claim that they had never failed to secure a gold in the Six-Day Trial since first competing in 1911.

On 6th September, H.F.S. put up such a fine performance in the Junior Car Club's General Efficiency Trial that there was a long delay before it could be decided whether he or Macklin in an Eric-Campbell should be awarded the Westall Cup. Sadly, the prize did eventually go to the Eric-Campbell. Nevertheless, the Morgan success was a useful one, for this trial was so designed as to prevent manufacturers tuning up their cars—the public could be sure that a standard machine was being used. This meant that coming second brought Morgans much favourable publicity.

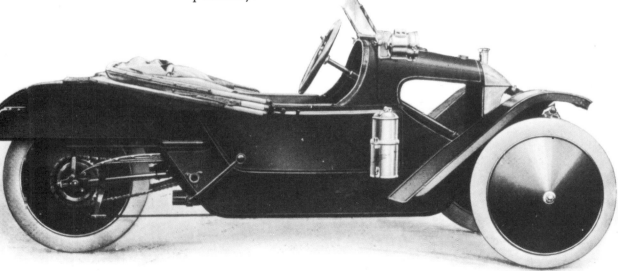

The 1918 Grand Prix model

The General Efficiency Trial awarded marks for low petrol consumption, hill-climbing ability, reliability over 60 miles, success in restarting on hills, silence, easy starting from cold, good acceleration, good braking, ability to run slowly and good steering control. H.F.S. made the most of his success by writing to *The Cyclecar*, pointing out how consistent it was that in spite of all the changes in the cyclecar world, Morgan had come second both in 1914 and 1919. This was indeed a case, he said, of survival of the fittest, for of the twenty-four makes which competed in 1914 only twelve still existed in 1919, although the list of entrants was swelled by the presence of five new names.

In August 1919, an article appeared in *The Cyclecar* about a special four-seater Morgan that had been built for Mr. E. B. Ware of J.A.P. In fact four-seater Morgans had existed since 1915, although the magazine rightly commented that Morgans did not list such a model in their catalogue. Nevertheless, no one was very surprised when a four-seater was displayed on the Morgan stand at the 1919 Show.

By early October 1919, the new Morgan factory was fully operational and for the first time the firm had the capacity to build 2,500 cars per year, although shortage of engines kept the numbers down for the time being.

Morgan successes in France began again in 1919, the most notable being Paul Houel's victory in the Circuit de L'Eure on 16th August. This had a considerable impact on the sales of the French-produced Morgan which came out later in the year and was called the Darmont Morgan.

The last important event for Morgans in 1919 was the London to Exeter run in which they once again took a gold medal. The winning driver was W. Pattison, and it must have been a great disappointment to the other Morgan entrant, L. J. D. Chapman, to learn that he too would have won a gold medal if he had not been observed arriving too early at a secret check-point.

At the end of the war, Brooklands was left in such poor condition that although some competitions were held elsewhere in the spring of 1919, none were held there. But Brooklands was not idle and workmen toiled throughout the year to try to restore the surface to something like its original condition. It must have been very pleasing to Morgans to come first and second in their first appearance at the circuit since 1914. The winning driver was the celebrated E. B. Ware with his single-seater racing Morgan. As I have said, Mr. Ware was head of the experimental department at

J.A.P., so it was not surprising that his car sported some interesting modifications, not the least of which was its Grand Prix style radiator which had been cut in half, reduced in size, and joined together again. The runner-up in this event was W. D. Hawkes in his M.A.G.-engined Morgan. The race took place at Easter in 1920 and this success, combined with a resounding Morgan victory in the London to Land's End trial must indeed have caused happy Easter feelings at Malvern. In the latter competition, Morgans carried off the Pettyt Cup and two gold medals in the passenger machine class.

In late February 1920, H.F.S. won the prize for the best three-wheeler in the Colmore cup competition and delighted the crowd by repeating one of his greatest feats, well remembered by enthusiasts since the last time he had performed it in 1913: being on the point of tipping over in spite of his passenger's weight being applied in the opposite direction, H.F.S. saved himself from disaster with a good push on the ground with his gauntleted right hand.

Another resounding Morgan success in 1920 came in the London to Edinburgh trial, held in May. Of the 282 motor-cycles, sidecars and three-wheelers entered, seven were Morgans and they won five gold medals and one silver between them.

By mid-1920 it was becoming clear that the staying power of cyclecars, with the exception of the Morgan, was on the decline, and from this time on an ever-decreasing number of cyclecars was seen in mixed motor-cycle and cyclecar competitions. But this did not deter Morgans. Although only four cyclecars were entered in the Scottish Six-Day Trial, two of them were Morgans, driven by H. B. Denley and H. F. Barge respectively. The latter unfortunately had to retire on the second day, so that the only gold medal going to a cyclecar was won by Denley in his M.A.G. Grand Prix model.

In July the first post-war French Grand Prix was held. As the course at Amiens was in a poor state of repair, the event was switched to a triangle of roads outside Le Mans where two of the three corners were altered and improved to make higher speeds possible. The favourite English competitor at this event was E. B. Ware in his special Morgan, but he was hit by bad luck. The reports vary enormously but probably the most reliable appeared in *The Motor Cycle*. In this account we are told that Ware soon settled down to second place behind M. Violet driving his Major cyclecar. (In 1913 he had been making the

Violet-Bogey but now called his cars Major.) Speeds well in excess of 70 m.p.h. were not uncommon in the race so it was not entirely surprising that after six laps of the 17.5-km. course Ware's engine began to overheat. He therefore pulled into the pits where the radiator was topped up. Unfortunately, when the cool water came into contact with the overheated engine it cracked the sleeve of one cylinder. It was also found that one of the chains needed replacing. However, in spite of the cracked cylinder Ware decided to continue the race. The impressive little J.A.P. could still bowl the car along at 40 m.p.h., even when running on only one cylinder, although the final result was that M. Violet had an easy win.

When the table of entries for the A.C.U. Six-Day Trial was published in August, Morgans proved to be the only cyclecars entered. Five Morgans were listed, of which those driven by H.F.S., James and Boddington were fitted with four speeds. They did not, of course, have special four-speed gearboxes, but instead had a two-speed box situated just behind the engine, in addition to the two rear dog clutches. On the first day, Mr. S. Hall caused a great sensation by succeeding in climbing Park Rash Hill in his Morgan. Seventy-five per cent of the motor-cyclists failed on this, and even H.F.S. failed in spite of the vigorous bouncing which was a well-known technique of his and other Morgan-ists. It is possible that Boddington might have succeeded but, unfortunately, his low-drive chain broke. Once again there were complaints from many competitors and so the worst hill on Wednesday's run was cut out by the stewards late on Tuesday night. Boddington was disqualified on Wednesday for arriving one and a quarter hours late at the lunch stop, partly because he obliged the solo-machine riders by letting them get ahead of him up Summer Lodge Hill. In view of these circumstances he decided to remain in the trial despite his disqualification. In the final part of the test, which was held at Brooklands, cars were required to go down the test hill at a speed of less than 10 m.p.h. The Morgans had a little difficulty in gripping on the concrete but nevertheless all was well, and in the end the Morgan team—H.F.S., F. James and S. Hall—all gained gold medals.

As usual the London to Exeter trial enabled Morgans to end the year with a flourish. Seven cars were entered (none of them works cars or works drivers) and four of them came home with gold medals and three with silver.

Apart from the racing successes, 1920 was a particularly significant year for Morgans in another direction. The car had changed remarkably little in its basic design over the years—probably the war was largely responsible for this. Furthermore, as I have said, the war years, with their lack of motor-racing, had caused the sporting journals to fill up their pages with articles suggesting how cyclecars could be improved. The 1921 model Morgans, announced in late 1920, clearly showed that H.F.S. had learned something from these suggestions. For the first time the back wheel could be detached without removing the drive chains. All that was now necessary was to slacken off the axle nuts, disconnect the band brakes (part of the new design was a feature making this operation simpler) and slide the axle forward and out. An improved bearing served as the hinge for the back fork and flat wooden guards were fitted to prevent mud from getting on to the chains.

Another improvement was effected by altering the sprocket sizes on the bevel box and back wheel, so that the two drive-chains became of equal length and hence interchangeable. Whenever the back wheel was removed the two chains could be swapped around and so made to wear more evenly. Other advantages resulting from this were that it became possible to fit a larger band brake on the high-speed side, and that it was hereafter only necessary to carry one spare drive-chain instead of two.

The front end of the car, too, had come in for a number of improvements—larger hubs were fitted for the first time, running on $\frac{3}{8}$-in. balls in the bearings, and an improved starting-handle mechanism was fitted. Beyond that the clutch withdrawal mechanism was redesigned and greatly improved and simplified (on the whole most of H.F.S.'s improvements were simplifications too!). The new method made it very much quicker to remove the engine and to attend to the clutch. Another innovation was that dynamo lighting became available as a standard extra, at a price of £25. A pulley was fitted to the flywheel and a Whittle belt drove the dynamo, which was fitted to the near-side chassis tube just behind the engine. The new improvements were widely acclaimed and, as had so often happened before, the entire estimated output for 1921 had been booked by November 1920.

So far, I have mentioned most of the more important Morgan victories of each year so that the reader will have some idea of the general context in which they were won. Brian Watts, celebrated historian of the three-wheeler club, has told me that just to make a brief mention of all the races in which Morgan three-wheelers were involved would fill many volumes. I therefore feel obliged, though rather

reluctantly, only to refer to those events which seem of outstanding interest in the remaining years of the history. The
vast number of events mentioned in the Morgan Archives
make any attempt to do otherwise impossible.

The end of the First World War had seen a feverish period
of car buying, but this boom was short-lived and pressure
began to fall off in the spring of 1921. Although Morgan was
almost completely unaffected by this slump, their prices
had to come down and, just to be quite sure of a safe place
in the cheap car market, H.F.S. decided to reintroduce the
Standard Popular model at the 1921 Show. This sold for
£150 at a time when all the other Morgan models cost about
£200. The Standard model was the original cheap two-
seater car of 1911, but after a few years all mention of the
name had disappeared from the catalogues. It was typical
of H.F.S. to find a way to cut the cost without cutting the
quality, and Mr. Watts has discovered that he was able to do
so by purchasing a bulk lot of French black poplar wood from
which the body was made. The car was slightly shorter than
other models at the time and its 8-h.p. J.A.P. air-cooled
engine gave it a top speed of 50 m.p.h. To compensate for
the slight loss of stability caused by the shorter length of the
car, the track was widened.

The new model was received with considerable enthusiasm. In an article about the 1921 Motor Cycle Show,
Motor Cycling commented: 'The new Morgans were specially
attractive and made one wonder if it is not a little silly to go
sliding about in the rain when a good, kind designer has gone
to the trouble of protecting the driver so thoroughly.'
Another magazine was pleased to report that no vital sacri-
fice had been made to lower the car's price and that all
important parts were the same as on the De Luxe model.

The Morgan team for the A.C.U. Stock Car Trial, March 1921

The Morgan team for the A.C.U. Six-Day Trial, August 1922

Morgan's greatest prestige-winning event in 1922 must have been the A.C.U. one-day trial for stock cars. The A.C.U. took great care to ensure that none of the cars and motor-cycles entered in this event had been tampered with in any way. All the machines had to come out of stocks held by agents, and once entered in the competition no tuning or modification of any sort was allowed. The purpose of the event was to show which machines, in the form available to prospective purchasers in the shops, could put up the best performance. The trial, which was held on 15th March, began at the Wolseley Motor Company's works in Birmingham and led via Kenilworth and Warwick to Oxford—a distance of 79 miles including some hill work such as Sun Rising Hill outside Kineton. A lunch stop was made at Oxford, after which competitors set off on the 63-mile drive to Brooklands, which included a second hill test at Kop near Princes Risborough. A speed trial was held at Brooklands, and to H.F.S.'s enormous delight all six Morgan entrants gained full marks and were given special certificates of merit. The Morgan drivers included H.F.S. and George Goodall, who was Morgans' works manager—and father of the present works manager. The triumph was all the greater because no other cyclecar won a single award as high as that won by each of the Morgans.

April brought some important new Brooklands records for Ware in his J.A.P.-engined Morgan. He broke the flying five mile record at 83.6 m.p.h. and the standing-start ten miles at 79.26 m.p.h.

1922 was also the year in which Anzani-engined Morgans first began to make a name for themselves. In June, Harry Martin came first in the five-lap passenger handicap at Brooklands at 70.58 m.p.h., and then second in a two-lap passenger handicap. British Anzani were not slow to advertise their Morgan successes. In August, a Morgan-Anzani driven by Carr was one of the gold-medal-winning Morgans in the A.C.U. Six-Day Trial, making the fastest climb on Bwlch-y-Groes test hill. Carr came second overall in the trial—he even beat H.F.S. who was driving his J.A.P.-engined machine. This success, in a field of 142 starters, was truly remarkable. The other two Morgans also did extremely well so that the trio ended up by gaining fourteen more marks than any other team entered. It was only because the three were not officially entered as a team that they did not obtain the team prize.

When the Motor Cycle Show was held in November, the Morgan stand was a centre of attraction, and when Sir Harold Bowden took the Duke of York on a tour of the show he began by showing him the Morgans. Here the pièce de résistance was an Anzani-engined Aero Morgan with the body finished in nickel plate with black wings. The Duke, we are told, was much impressed by it, but perhaps this is understandable since he himself owned a Morgan-Anzani. Another reason for popular interest was that prices were again down: the Standard model cost only £128 and, like all the other models, was now offered for the first time with a Blackburne engine as an alternative to the J.A.P. The Family model was offered at £158 water-cooled or £148 air-cooled, and the Grand Prix at £155. The Anzani engine used in the Aero model was an o.h.v. water-cooled 8-h.p. unit with a water-heated induction pipe.

Apart from the advent of Anzani and Blackburne engines, however, there was very little alteration in the Morgans at the Show and it was not until the spring of 1923 that we find such remarkable innovations as the availability of front-wheel brakes as an optional extra. Despite the lack of change, all reviews of the 1923 models were very favourable. *The Motor Cycle* said: 'Fascinating in its admirable simplicity, the Morgan must take pride of place. It stands in a class by itself,' and *Auto* said: 'It can be relied on to go anywhere.' Perhaps it would be impossible to be unenthusiastic about a car which, in 1922 alone, won ten silver cups for reliability, nine special certificates of merit, thirty-seven gold medals and took the world records for 1 km., 5 miles and 10 miles for two-seaters under 1,100 c.c.

The first announcement of front-wheel braking came in *The Cyclecar* of 30th March 1923, although a number of customers had already had this luxury fitted to their cars. Morgans had spent over two years perfecting the mechanism, yet even now it had to be worked independently from the rear brakes by a hand lever. It was still considered that the extra stopping power should only be needed in an emergency. Needless to say, one of the first Morgans to be fitted with these brakes was E. B. Ware's Standard model and they were well demonstrated in his excellent performance in the Junior Car Club Efficiency Trial. The front brake drums, described as not being large or unsightly, were linked to the lever by Bowden cables and, if properly adjusted, could be relied upon to give very even stopping power. This new optional extra was available for all models at a cost of £6.

Extras Available for 1923

	£.	s.	d.
Disc wheel covers	3.	0.	0.
Tubes filled with Impirvo (each)		7.	6.
Hood Cover	1.	0.	0.
Painting Numbers		5.	0.
Watch (eight-day)	3.	0.	0.
Speed Indicator (Cowey)	5.	5.	0.
Colours: grey, red, blue or purple except Standard model			
Other colours	2.	0.	0.
Four-speed gear	10.	0.	0.
Lucas Electric Light set	10.	0.	0.
Brakes on front wheels hand operated	6.	0.	0.
10-h.p. British Anzani Engines (o.h.v. with aluminium pistons and mechanical oil pumps)	5.	0.	0.
M.A.G. engines	5.	0.	0.

1923 was also an historic year in that the total number of Morgans in circulation, including several hundred Darmont Morgans which had been made under licence in France, reached the 40,000 mark. Thus it is not surprising that H.F.S. was obliged to extend his factory quite considerably that year to cope with the ever-increasing demand. Once again H.F.S. gave a party in the new buildings which was attended by some 500 people. In his speech he said he had

wondered, when the first extension had opened three years
previously, whether it would be too large. The fact that even
larger works were now needed was entirely thanks to his
men who, instead of slacking or striking as the business had
expanded, had all pulled together. The extensions enabled
the whole factory to be united at last under one roof.

E. B. Ware with his mechanic, Mr. Allchin, in March 1923

Undoubtedly the most exciting single day that year was the day in March when E. B. Ware won the much-coveted Westall Cup, which H.F.S. had only just missed in 1922, in the Junior Car Club's General Efficiency Trial. On the same day the Morgan team in the Victory Cup Trial won the Watsonian Cup for the best team performance of any kind of machine. Ware's victory was very impressive—he gained 1,743 marks out of a possible 2,000, his nearest competitor gaining 1,666. He made the fastest time of the day in the hill-climb and came first in both the top gear acceleration test and the standing start acceleration test. It is a remarkable tribute to the car that the former time was 9 secs. for 100 yards and the latter 8.4. All this was achieved not on one of Mr. Ware's specially hotted-up machines but on an ordinary Standard model. Ware also proved the success of Morgan's researches into front-wheel braking by pulling up in the shortest time on the 1-in-5 test hill—4 yards. One interesting innovation in the trial was a suspension test, in which cars were required to drive over a 2 in. plank of wood at 25 m.p.h. while a film was made. Unfortunately history does not relate how the Morgan fared in this part of the trial.

Finally, 1923 was remarkable for the large number of British and world records broken by Morgans; especially those won by G. N. Norris, a hitherto unknown Morganist who rose to fame in a single day at Brooklands by expert handling of his Blackburne-engined Morgan. On 10th October he won the flying five miles and the standing-start ten miles records; then, on 6th November, he won the flying kilometre and flying mile records for his class.

Another successful record breaker was W. D. Hawkes who used his Anzani-engined Morgan in the class for single-seater cyclecars under 1,100 c.c. In September he set up several new records, including a new world record for the flying mile at a mean speed of 90.38 m.p.h. and the British flying kilometre (one-way) at 92.17 m.p.h. In addition to these successes E. B. Ware set up four new records for 750-c.c. single-seaters at Brooklands in June, and Poiret set up a flying kilometre record in the Bois de Boulogne. Altogether, by the end of the year Morgans had taken fourteen places in the table of world and British records for 1923. The speed was truly remarkable, but with it the danger increased until it brought on some serious trouble in the next year. But more of that later.

1924 brought the second consecutive Westall Cup win for E. B. Ware and his Morgan and it was particularly satisfactory that another Morgan, driven by G. N. Norris, should

The Family model, 1925

have come third, although the whole field was down to only fourteen cars. Between them the two Morgan drivers came first in seven of the nine tests and only did badly in the easy-starting and slow-running-in-top-gear tests. But the year was by no means one of plain sailing for Ware and his Morgan, and in September disaster struck. The competition concerned was the International 200-mile Light Car Race held at Brooklands. Throughout the race, both Ware and Norris were plagued by bad luck. Even as the cars were starting off Ware's engine failed to pick up properly and he was left at the back of the field. After a few laps he was in even more serious trouble, and on pulling into the pits found he had broken his top-gear dog. In spite of his disappointment on discovering the gravity of his trouble, he set to work to mend the car. It cost him several laps. While all this was going on G. N. Norris was having a terrific battle for third place with Zborowski in a Salmson, finally succeeding in passing him at the tenth lap. Meanwhile, having repaired his top-gear dog, Ware was back in the race, but soon he was again reported missing and a few minutes later was to be seen pushing his car into the pits, closely followed by Beart in another Morgan. Beart had a flat rear tyre and while he and his supporters were struggling to mend his car, Norris came freewheeling into the pits with a broken top-gear chain, thus putting all three Morgans out of action at the same time. The only encouragement at this moment came when O. Wilson-Jones, who had been leading the race from the start in his Salmson, also came into the pits. But the optimism in the Morgan camp soon faded when they realized that only a fill of water was needed and the Salmson roared off within a few moments.

Soon the first of the three crippled Morgans was ready to start off again—Beart had his new tyre securely in place, but when he and his mechanic began to push the car away to start it, they could not get it to fire. They tried again twice but without success, and the car had to be further attended to before it could get back into the race. In the meantime Norris' chain was ready and so off he went, although he was so far behind that he obviously had no chance of doing at all well. Ware too was soon on his way again and it seemed that his luck had taken a turn for the better—his car was now consistently lapping at almost 90 m.p.h. When Ware had completed his thirty-third lap some of the spectators began to cast anxious glances at his rear wheel and he too was seen to be glancing behind him from time to time. There could be no doubt that it was wobbling quite badly, and Thomas reported afterwards that he had smelled burning rubber when passing Ware in his Thomas-Special at this time. On its thirty-fifth lap Ware's car was seen to swerve suddenly across the track in a sickening fashion. It then skidded, crashed into the corrugated iron fence, and finally spun round, hurling Ware and his mechanic Allchin into the air. The former landed on the grass; the latter was less fortunate and came to rest on the concrete. An appeal was immediately put out on the loudspeakers for a doctor and both men were rushed to hospital while numerous officials risked their lives to try to clear the track of debris and avoid a further accident. Both men recovered but Ware never raced again, and the race organizers had received a shock from which they could not recover—a shock that was to have far-reaching effects for Morgans in the future.

It seems that many people in the racing world had it in for three-wheelers in one way or another, and they therefore seized on the opportunity presented by Ware's crash to have them banned from competitive racing. Perhaps people had come to feel that no one else had much chance of winning the Westall Cup while Morgans were allowed to compete.

The Junior Car Club, supported by the Brooklands authorities, therefore banned three-wheelers from the J.C.C. High Speed Efficiency Trial and the 200-mile race. In March 1925, George Morgan wrote to *The Cyclecar* and pointed out that it was a little odd that the J.C.C.—originally the Cyclecar Club—should no longer admit to membership owners of the one surviving cyclecar. He also said that in view of the opinion of many competitors as quoted in the *J.C.C. Gazette* of April 1924—namely that 'a three-wheeler was bound to win the Westall Cup'—he was not surprised at the decision to ban Morgans. The secretary of the J.C.C. said: 'It was decided that on grounds of safety it was not advisable to allow vehicles having only three wheels to run in the trial.'

Charles Laff of the French d'Yrsan cyclecar company took up the cry against the J.C.C., and said in a letter to *The Cyclecar*: 'The one and only accident to Mr. Ware is not a reasonable basis for the J.C.C.'s decision, as it should remember that there have been many accidents to four-wheel cars at Brooklands. If the J.C.C. is going to ban one car after another through accidents, we can see the "200" being held as a cycle race in the not too distant future.'

But all was not lost by a long chalk—the Morgan could still take part in most trials and rallies and could also break records. In August, W. A. Carr was the only three-wheeler entrant in the A.C.U. International Six-Day Trial. In its summary of the event, *The Motor Cycle* said: 'A brilliant performance by the only three-wheeler entrant; he lost one time-mark only and climbed all hills splendidly. His passenger deserves special praise.'

Morgans also made many outstanding contributions to world records in the three-wheeler class.* In this respect, H. Beart began to steal the limelight from Norris in 1925 when he broke a total of thirteen records, including the flying kilometre at 103.77 m.p.h. and the flying mile at 102.65 m.p.h. Furthermore, in the one hour continuous run he succeeded in covering 91.48 miles. Thus despite the restriction Morgans could feel quite proud of themselves at the end of 1925.

Beart's record-breaking Morgan had a number of interesting modifications which helped it to achieve such outstanding victories. The chassis-frame was strengthened to withstand the strains to which it was subjected at these

* The class was for three-wheel cyclecars, with passenger, having a capacity of not more than 1,100 c.c.

H. Beart in his Blackburne-engined Morgan, 1925

very high speeds, and the rear quarter elliptic springs were each fitted with seven leaves of graduated thickness. A single Hartford shock-absorber was mounted over the rear wheel and with considerable ingenuity Beart had also succeeded in fitting shock-absorbers to the front suspension. The steering had been modified, too, spring-loaded ball-joints being used for the track-rod connections, and it was geared down by the use of Ford epicyclic steering reduction gears fitted to the top of the column. Further peculiarities of his car were that only front-wheel brakes were fitted and these were controlled by a hand-lever outside the body: there was no footbrake at all. To facilitate changing up, a push-button switch was fitted to the top of the gear lever and connected to the magneto. Thus, when changing gear there was no need to slip the clutch or alter the throttle opening. Pressure on the button whilst the lever was moved from one position to another allowed the engine to slow down momentarily and cut in again the instant the gear was home. The gear ratios were so devised that at 100 m.p.h. the Blackburne engine was turning over at 4,300 r.p.m. No attempt was made to cut down the weight of the car—it was probably heavier than some other racing Morgans, but Mr. Beart thought that reasonable weight added to efficiency by helping the machine to hold the track. The fact that the car could be driven at 90 m.p.h. with no hands on the wheel would seem to prove this point.

A further ban, imposed in the spring of 1926, also had some significance for Morgans for it was at this time that the Motor Cycling Club decided to ban its trade members from competing in its trials. Thus, H.F.S. was hereafter rather

THE MOTOR CYCLE

3ᴰ

"Make it a Morgan Holiday"

Why stay at home and envy your friends who get out every holiday, every week-end? You can get away to the seaside too—as inexpensively, as comfortably, as surely, as satisfactorily —by Morgan. The Morgan Runabout costs much less than a car, yet gives the same performance. Its tax is only £4, its petrol consumption 50 m.p.g., its speed 60 m.p.h., there are only three tyres to maintain, and the Morgan is simple to handle, easy to understand.

Ask for our new Folder illustrating the 1926 models at prices from £95. Get YOUR Morgan and let the other fellows envy YOU

The Morgan Motor Co. Ltd., Malvern Link, Worcs.

Standard . . . £95
Family Model . £116
Tax only . . £4
Petrol . . 50 m.p.g.

Morgan Runabout

"The Pioneer & still the best"

The Morgan was the forerunner of the "economy light car" movement and is still miles ahead of any.

A new style in advertising—June 1926

restricted in the events in which he could compete. Perhaps as a result of the impending ban, the entry for the London to Land's End trial (this was the last trial before the ban came into effect) was an all-time record of 530. H.F.S. was not among the record number of sixteen Morgans which entered, although he can scarcely have failed to be pleased by the four gold, six silver and one bronze medals that they won. This was a fine result considering that on test hills such as Porlock, three-wheelers were required to maintain the same average speed as two-litre cars.

Perhaps the second greatest Morgan achievement in 1926 was that obtained in the A.C.U. International Six-Day Trial, when the Morgan team, consisting of W. Carr, G. H. Goodall and R. T. Horton, all gained gold medals and easily carried off the team prize. In fact they only lost 20 marks between them while the nearest rival—the only side-car team to survive the trial—lost a total of 310.

In November, Morgans continued their well-tried policy of adding small technical refinements to their cars for the Motor Cycle Show, without in any way altering the basic lay-out or appearance. The result was successful. The chassis of the De Luxe, Family and Aero models were lengthened and widened to give a little extra room for the driver and passengers, and 7-in. diameter front-wheel brakes were fitted. Also fitted as standard were 4-in. Dunlop tyres and grease-gun lubrication. The rear hub was enlarged and the counter-shaft, back axle and dogs were all strengthened. The seats were 3 in. longer than in previous years, but because of the longer chassis there was still 3 in. extra leg-room. Finally, the internal appearance of the cars was smartened up with mottled aluminium dashboards.

I mentioned earlier that the Motor Cycling Club decided to ban trade entries in its trials. It is therefore interesting to note that the consequences of this were not exactly grave for Morgans. No less than 21 Morgans were entered for the 1926 London to Exeter trial at Christmas 1926 and of these a total of 11 won gold medals, and 3 won silvers.

Morgans scored a very spectacular success in the 1927 London to Edinburgh when, of the 14 starters, 11 won gold medals and the remaining 3 all won silvers. However, the year was chiefly significant for the resurrection of great enthusiasm in three-wheeler racing. The movement began when two anonymous contributors to *The Cyclecar*, who adopted the pseudonyms of 'Shacklepin' and 'Grand Prix', complained that there had been a partial collapse of enthusiasm and opportunity for three-wheeler owners to

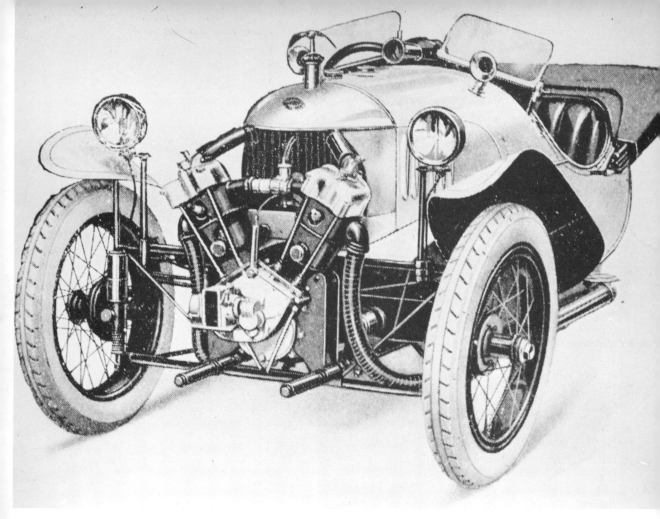

The Blackburne-engined Aero of 1926

race since the J.C.C. had banned them from its events at Brooklands late in 1924. They called on the three-wheeler world to do something about this. The result was a great flood of correspondence which led to the Morgan Club's deciding in August to reconstitute itself as the new Cyclecar Club and open its doors to all cyclecar owners, although only four-wheelers of up to 1,100 c.c. would be allowed to compete against the three-wheelers in races. Everyone was anxious to dispel the old rumour that three-wheelers were dangerous, that they skidded easily and that punctures could be disastrous. It was sad and ironic that one of the most outspoken men on this matter—J. J. Hall—had a serious crash in his Morgan at Brooklands, resulting from a rear-wheel puncture at 90 m.p.h., only a few weeks after publishing a letter in which he stated that he had covered more than 1,600 miles at Brooklands at high speeds without ever having the slightest anxiety about crashing. Nevertheless, the new Cyclecar Club went ahead and, aided by such capable men as H. Beart and Professor Low, devised some good plans for 1928.

Morgans brought in some quite important innovations late in 1927 for their 1928 models. The use of self-starters was becoming quite regular on Morgans now* and all 1928 models were fitted with a new type of dynamo drive taken from the bevel-box counter-shaft. The Standard model was given something of a front-end face-lift and although it was not ready in time for the Show a steering reduction gear of 2 to 1 was announced. A new model of the Family type became available with a detachable van body, and perhaps more significantly the Super Sports Aero was announced, which later became known simply as the 'Super Sports'. This car had a chassis 6 in. longer and $2\frac{1}{2}$ in. lower than previous Aero models, and was fitted with the latest J.A.P. 10–40-h.p. LTOWC engine. Its price was £150 which, considering its 80 m.p.h. top speed, was not at all bad.

As usual the London–Exeter produced a happy note on which to end the year. While the motoring journals headed their articles with captions such as 'Few gold medals in the Exeter', no less than eight Morgan owners returned home with beaming faces knowing that they were among those few.

By far the most important event of the 1928 Morgan year was the long-awaited new Cyclecar Club's Grand Prix, which was held at Brooklands in August. The event was open to all cars, both three- and four-wheelers, having a capacity of not more than 1,100 c.c. While a dozen Morgans formed a significant part of the entry, there were numerous other makes represented including Coventry-Victor, Amilcar, Salmson, Austin, Riley and Jowett. The meeting began with a two-lap Novices' handicap which was won by Maj. Gardner in his supercharged Salmson, and this was followed by three other minor races which were all won by Morgans, the drivers being Horton (twice) and R. R. Jackson. The final race was the main event: the 50-mile Cyclecar Grand Prix. Entries for this race were divided into three classes: (a) under 850 c.c. (b) 850–1,100 c.c. (c) supercharged up to 1,100 c.c. In fact the third class only had one entrant and that was Maj. Gardner's Salmson. He unfortunately fractured a petrol pipe in the second lap and had to retire. Many people had predicted that the return of three-wheeler

* They had been offered since 1926.

Grand Prix racing would bring a wave of accidents but, in fact, the only accident of the day involved a four-wheeler. In the second lap of the Grand Prix, E. Martin had a narrow escape at the first S-bend in his Austin and then crashed into one of the sand banks round which competitors were required to weave their way. His car overturned, throwing him out, and he was rushed to hospital but happily suffered nothing worse than a broken arm. In the sixth lap Horton, who had astonished everyone by lapping at 98 m.p.h. in his Morgan-Blackburne in one of the earlier races, had to retire with brake trouble. At this time Clive Lones was lying third behind an Austin and a Coventry-Victor, and he now began to put on the pressure. By the seventeenth lap he was in the lead in his Morgan-J.A.P. He finally won the race by a one-lap lead and enjoyed the rare honour of winning three classes simultaneously.

The success of the event was widely acclaimed and people were much impressed by the safety with which three-wheelers could be raced at speeds up to 100 m.p.h. Nor was it forgotten that three-wheelers had won four of the five races that day. It is difficult to say exactly what was the secret of Lones' success in the Grand Prix, but perhaps it had something to do with the fact that his mechanic was his wife!

THE TWO-SEATER THEY TALK ABOUT BEFORE MARRIAGE— AND THE ONE THEY GET!

Cartoon, circa *1926*

Back in 1922, a woman motor-cyclist called Mrs. Gwenda Stewart made her début at Brooklands and succeeded in breaking a number of records in the 250-c.c. class before going off to Alaska for a few years. By the time she returned in 1925, women had been banned from motor-cycling at Brooklands, and so she began to break records at Montlhéry. She did so with remarkable success until 1927, when her rear wheel buckled and caused her to crash. The accident prompted her to move from motor-cycles to three-wheelers and in September 1928 she won a number of world records in the 750-c.c. three-wheeler class, driving a J.A.P.-engined M.E.B. three-wheeler. When these records were snatched away from her in November by H. Beart in his Morgan, she began to feel that 'if you can't lick 'em—join 'em' was the best policy for her. Beart had raised Gwenda Stewart's hour record from 74.19 miles to 82.38 in one attempt, and this undoubtedly impressed her. Hereafter, she was to be a most valuable asset to the Morgan cause.

When the Motor Cycle Show opened at Olympia in November 1928, it was revealed that only two makes of cyclecar were present: Morgan and Coventry-Victor. Both H.F.S. and Mr. Weaver of Coventry-Victor lamented this, as they felt that a little more competition could only do good to the three-wheeler cause. Nevertheless the two stands were well worth seeing, and visitors to the Morgan stand learned that a number of improvements had been made to the 1929 models. The bearings of the rear hub and bevel box were fitted with oil-retaining felt washers, and geared steering (which had been available on 1928 models at extra cost) now became standard. The dynamo drive was improved by the fitting of helical gears and the sliding axles on the front suspension were provided with a grease cavity.

The 1928 Show saw the passing of the Standard model, the cheapest two-seater machine now being the De Luxe. This had a new type of body on a long chassis and was priced, like the Family model, at £92. These non-sports models all had air-cooled J.A.P. engines of 980 c.c. Front-wheel brakes were standard on all Morgans for 1929 except the cheapest De Luxe model, and electric starters could be fitted to any model for £8, although they needed some assistance on frosty mornings.

By far the hottest car in the Morgan range was the Super Sports Aero which cost £150. This car would hold its own as regards acceleration to about 60 m.p.h. with almost any car on the road, including Bentleys, and its top speed, even without special tuning, was over 80 m.p.h. It had

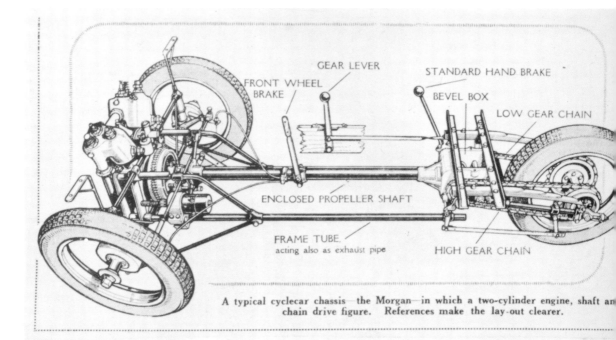

A typical cyclecar chassis the Morgan in which a two-cylinder engine, shaft an
chain drive figure. References make the lay-out clearer.

The Morgan chassis, circa *1927*

shock-absorbers fitted both front and rear, and to give it greater stability its track was wider than on the other models. The engine was an o.h.v. water-cooled J.A.P. of 1,096 c.c. Another factor which gave it greater stability was that although it used the same chassis as the ordinary Aero, it was set $2\frac{1}{2}$ in. lower. The smart tail was hinged to give easy access to the rear wheel, the oil tank that lubricated the chains, and the battery.

The success of the new Cyclecar Club's first Grand Prix was only equalled by the same event in 1929, and this time all five races were won by Morgans. The two-lap Novices' race was won from two Austins by S. Allard in his Morgan at 73.37 m.p.h., and T. A. Rhodes won the three-wheeler handicap in spite of being up against such tough opposition as R. T. Horton and Clive Lones. In the third race, in spite of the presence of four supercharged cars (Austin, Ratier, Salmson and Amilcar), nothing seemed able to catch the Morgans, and Horton won with Lones not far behind. In the fourth race, only three of the seven starters finished— Rhodes in his Morgan (the winner) and two Austins.

When the Grand Prix was announced, special artificial bends had been prepared in the final stretch of the course to keep drivers on their toes. Twenty-one cars started and those whose capacity was under 850 c.c. were credited with three laps. On the first lap one of the Amilcars collided at the paddock bend and burst a tyre. The driver replaced the wheel but on the second lap collided again at the same place and retired. While all this was going on, no one was paying much attention to C. Jay in his works 750-c.c. Morgan-J.A.P. He was driving in a good steady way so that it was not until people checked on the scoreboard that they were aware of what a skilful race this young driver was running. He continued to drive in the same intelligent if unspectacular way for the rest of the race and soon had a lead of two laps over his nearest rival, Maj. Gardner in his Amilcar. It was a fine performance and he was a worthy winner. It was the first time that the Morgan world had really heard of Mr. Jay as a driver, although he was well-known as the stores manager of Morgans. Today we all know him as the friendly service director.

Police work in a Morgan—1929

As I mentioned before, Gwenda Stewart saw the light and joined the Morgan camp at the end of 1928. Accordingly, at the beginning of 1929, she approached Douglas Hawkes and asked him to prepare a car for her. Hawkes used an almost standard Morgan Super Sports model and fitted a 994-c.c. J.A.P. o.h.v. air-cooled engine. He prepared the car and engine with incredible thoroughness to make sure that there would be maximum reliability. Mrs. Stewart was also able to benefit from Hawkes' great experience in the technique of Morgan record-breaking from the driving point of view. They made an ideal team, and at their first attempt, which was on the 5-km. and 5-mile records, she succeeded in breaking both at speeds in excess of 103 m.p.h. By the end of the year she had broken literally dozens of records, using the same car but with different sizes of J.A.P. engines. She even succeeded in covering 101.5 miles in one hour, which was universally regarded as an outstanding feat. In point of fact she only just made it, for she ran out of petrol on the very second in which the hour ended. She was certainly a brave girl, for the Montlhéry track is on top of a hill (some say this is in order to prevent anyone having a free view!) with the result that winds were very often extremely strong and many attempts had to be made in wet and gusty conditions. Furthermore, the combination of the roughness of the track and the hardness of the Morgan suspension often resulted in her wearing holes in her overalls during record-breaking attempts!

1929 was really a remarkable year for Morgan world records, for while Gwenda was setting them up in the larger capacity classes at Montlhéry, Clive Lones was upholding the honour of the lower-powered Morgans at Brooklands. In October, using his 346-c.c. J.A.P.-engined Morgan, he raised the 5-km. (flying start) record in the 350-c.c. class from 68.15 m.p.h. to 70.47 m.p.h., and raised the hour record from 57.22 miles to 66.68. Beyond these he broke no less than six other world records.

It was only sad that this most successful year did not end on the note of triumph of so many previous years—in the London to Exeter. 1929 was one of the very few years in which Morgans won no gold medals at all in this trial. Of the ten starters, 3 won silver medals, 4 won bronzes and 3 retired.

1930 started off with some remarkable successes from Mrs. Stewart—the fastest female Morganist in the world. At Montlhéry she set up records for a 750-c.c. engine in her Morgan as follows: 5 km. at 95.81 m.p.h.; 5 miles at

95.52 m.p.h.; 10 km. at 88.46 m.p.h.; 10 miles at 91.07 m.p.h.

In May further feathers were added to her cap when she drove an 1,100-c.c. Morgan-J.A.P. at Montlhéry and covered 1,500 km. at 72.42 m.p.h.; 1,000 miles at 72.50; 2,000 km. at 71.63 m.p.h.; 2,500 km. at 71.50 m.p.h. In a twelve-hour period she covered 870.714 miles (an average of 72.55 m.p.h.) and in twenty-four hours 1,553.05 miles (64.71 m.p.h.). Her co-driver was S. C. H. Davis. The only reason for the twenty-four hours being slower was a breakdown at the twenty-second hour, otherwise this too would have been achieved at over 70 m.p.h.

In May 1930 *The Cyclecar* reviewed an Aero Morgan with the new M-type chassis, which had come out in October

Gwenda Stewart with Douglas Hawkes and her record-breaking Morgan

1929. It is amusing to notice how like many of the reviews of today's Morgans it sounds: 'There is and always has been something altogether delightful about a Morgan which defies definition. . . . There is, in the opinion of the writer, no independent standard with which the Morgan performance can be compared; a Morgan is a Morgan and it can be compared with nothing else but another Morgan. . . . As to performance—it is perhaps easier to say that it is typically "Morgan". Readers who have themselves driven these cyclecars will understand what is meant; those who have never sampled a Morgan have missed an interesting and instructive experience.'

The reviewer concluded that the Aero Morgan appealed to a vast crowd of young, moderately well-off people who had become tired of motor-cycles yet required a vehicle with a big reserve of power which only very highly priced sports cars and three-wheelers could give. He heartily praised the improved suspension and stability, and his only real criticism was against the hand-throttle whose replacement with an accelerator pedal, he thought, would make gear changing considerably easier.

In August the remarkable Mrs. Stewart really made the motoring world sit up when she broke four international records in a big way at Montlhéry, using an 1,100-c.c. Morgan-J.A.P. She covered 5 km. at 113.27 m.p.h. and 5 miles at 107.27 m.p.h. But still this amazing woman had not finished staggering the motoring world. At the end of August she drove the same car, but with a 750-c.c. J.A.P. engine, at 100.64 m.p.h.—the first time in history that such a small-engined car had exceeded the 100 mark. Just to give some idea of how hard Mrs. Stewart was working at this time I ought perhaps to point out that in the period from 1st January to 15th May 1930 she broke no less than 44 records! The highest speed she recorded came in the same year at Arpajon, where with the 1,100-c.c. J.A.P. back on the Morgan she covered the kilometre at a mean speed of 115.66 m.p.h.

The 1930 Motor Cycle Show saw few major changes in the Morgan range except that the bonnet of the Family model was redesigned and the price of the standard model went down to £85, or £90 with a water-cooled engine. An extra £10 bought an electric self-starter, a set of side screens and a speedometer. The Aero Morgan on a two-speed B-chassis began at £105, and the Family De Luxe model on an M-chassis at £90. The most expensive machine in the whole range was the Super Sports Aero model on an M-type chassis with a 10–40-h.p. J.A.P. engine, which with self-starter cost £145.

With the Great Depression of the early 1930s becoming ever more serious, prices had to drop still further in July 1931 so that the Standard Family model cost £75 or £80 water-cooled, the De Luxe Family model cost £80, and the prices of all other Morgans dropped by £10.

The first important Morgan success in 1931 came in April in the London to Land's End trial. 384 vehicles entered on this occasion and it was described as the most difficult run in memory. The Morgan entrants were therefore justly proud of the five gold and three silver medals they won.

In July the Light Car Club held its first Relay Grand Prix at Brooklands, which replaced the more conventional Grand Prix of previous years. Sadly, the Morgan team which comprised Lones, Maskell and Rhodes, was placed last. This was most unfair as it was entirely caused by the Morgans being given the smallest handicap—only 5 minutes as compared with as much as 54 minutes given to other teams. Lones was amazingly fast, lapping at speeds up to 92 m.p.h., often with at least one wheel in the air on the corners. In fact the overall average of the Morgan team was a very respectable 71.84 m.p.h. as compared with the 65.01 m.p.h. achieved by the winning team.

The Cyclecar was very sympathetic about the injustice suffered by the Morgans and finished its report on the event by saying: 'Better luck next time, Mr. Morgan.'

December brought as usual a good turnout of Morgans for the London to Exeter and, in fact, nine of the eleven three-wheelers entered were Morgans, the other two being B.S.A.s. The Morgans did very well, gaining five premier awards and three silvers, but this cannot be considered a particularly special achievement as conditions were very favourable and the surfaces of the observed hills were all good.

The autumn of 1931 saw the introduction of a new chassis with a gearbox which had three forward speeds and reverse. From this time on, only the Standard Family model and the Aeros were advertised as being available as two-speeders—others had the three-speed gearboxes and J.A.P. engines. At the same time electric starters, windscreen wipers and speedometers became standard equipment on all the three-speed models. The most expensive car in the whole range was the Super Sports at £145. This had a chassis $2\frac{1}{2}$ in. lower than usual, special front sliding axles, shock-absorbers in front and a high compression specially tuned o.h.v. 10–40 engine. Morgan's only competitor at the Motor Cycle Show in 1931 was Coventry-Victor. In spite of the depression which was in full swing at that time, *The Cyclecar* reported in December that both H.F.S. and Mr. Weaver of Coventry-Victor were delighted with the widespread interest taken in their stands.

The spring of 1932 saw the advent of another new model, called simply 'The Sports Two-Seater'. When *The Cyclecar* announced its appearance in May, it pointed out that it was destined to succeed the Aero model. As Mr. Watts has pointed out, this is why so few three-speed Aeros were ever produced.

The new car quite closely resembled the Aero model which it replaced, and in its normal form was fitted with only one door which was on the passenger's side. A second door could, however, be fitted to special order. Prospective buyers had a choice of windscreens with hoods to match: they could either take the Aero-style windscreen with a rounded top or have an ordinary flat one. The gearbox on this car was the first of the new leather-sealed type which did not drip oil like its predecessor. The Sports Two-Seater sold for £125 with an o.h.v. 10–40-h.p. water-cooled J.A.P. engine, although a side-valve engine was also available at a saving of £10. It was the first Morgan to be fitted with a single dry-plate clutch.

Back in the competition world, fourteen Morgans entered for the London to Edinburgh trial in May. This greatly pleased three-wheeler enthusiasts, since otherwise this type of car would not have been represented at all.

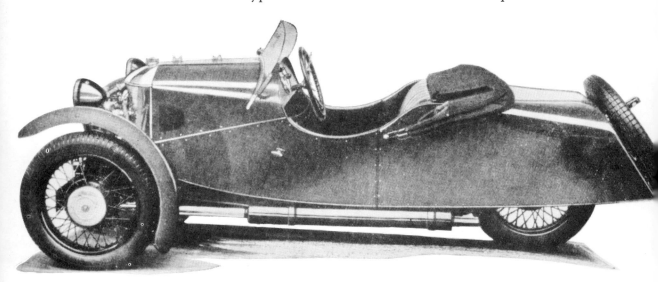

The 1933 model Sports two-seater—the first with detachable wheels

Three-wheeler supporters and especially Morgan enthusiasts had even more reason to be pleased when they learned that the Morgan had taken five premier awards and seven silver medals.

In July the Light Car Club held another Relay Grand Prix at Brooklands, where a total of twenty-nine teams entered as compared with twelve in 1931. Everyone was anxious to see how the specially prepared Morgans would fare against a team of very fast single-seater Austin Sevens. Unfortunately the Morgans met with even less success than in the previous year and the team was not even placed. It must have been some slight consolation to the drivers to learn that there was also no Austin in the first three teams to finish.

As there was no Motor Cycle Show in 1932, H.F.S. made up for it by putting on a special show and lunch in Malvern at which he exhibited eight models. It was sad that it was this particular year which lacked a Show as more changes than ever before had been incorporated in the Morgans.

For the first time the old two-speeder chassis was not mentioned in the catalogue, although a Family model with air-cooled engine, hood and electric light could be built to order for only £80. The new chassis could be supplied with four types of body: Super Sports, Sports Two-Seater, Sports Family and Family. Another significant change was to be found in the transmission: for their twenty-one years of existence Morgans had always used cone clutches, but these were now discontinued and replaced with single-plate dry clutches. The clutch pedal operated three toggle levers through the agency of a carbon block which required no lubrication. These levers in turn forced the two parts of the clutch apart against the springs. A number of modifications were carried out to the steering mechanism with the result that it became significantly lighter than previously. Until this time Morgans had used different chassis for Super Sports to those used on the other models. Now the chassis was standard throughout and a half-inch higher than the old Super Sports models. This meant that, with the exception of the Super Sports, all models were now lower than before. Dunlop Magna wheels were fitted for the first time, making the wheels removable and interchangeable, and new hubs were fitted to accommodate the new wheels. A spare wheel was fitted on the tail of all models. The reliability of the engine was still further improved by the fitting of a new type of water-proof distributor, and the gearbox (three-speed of course) was more oil-tight with its new type of seal.

The Super Sports was made a little wider at the front and the occupants were given more foot-room, while the appearance was enhanced by chromium-plated exhaust pipes which were carried back along the body. The Family model was completely redesigned to improve both its comfort and appearance. At this time all the Morgans were using J.A.P. engines, but in March 1933 the first Morgan Matchless came into production, using a Matchless water-cooled V-twin 50° engine of 990 c.c. with side valves, coil ignition and of course electric starter (although this did not always work on cold mornings!). The car which was very favourably reviewed in *The Cyclecar* in March 1933 was the Sports model and sold for £110. Its top speed was nearly 70 m.p.h. and 60 could be reached in 17 seconds from a standing start.

July 1933 at last brought a Morgan success in the Relay Grand Prix at Brooklands. Eighty-seven cars entered the 250-mile race and the Morgan team, whose drivers were Lones, Laird and Rhodes, came second at an average speed of 89.01 m.p.h. The winning team, the M.G. Car Club, only averaged 88.62 m.p.h., but as they had an eight-minute handicap they were placed first.

The rules of the race required each car in each team of three to attempt to cover one-third of the 250 miles. If a car was unable to complete its share, the next car could be sent out to cover its own stint and make up the balance. A sash was given to each team and this had to be carried in whichever car was currently in the race.

Retirements began within fifteen minutes of the start and before the race was over three complete teams and a total of twenty-four cars had had to withdraw. To give some idea of what was happening, the Wolseley Hornet team was down to its last car after only ten laps.

Although Rhodes' Morgan was lapping at speeds up to 102 m.p.h. the order after twenty laps was: first, M.G.; second, Singer; and third, Vale Special. With one hour ten minutes of the race gone, Rhodes began to develop engine trouble and so handed the sash to Laird. Although no Morgan was to be found among the first three cars at the sixty-lap stage, hope was by no means lost. The speed of the Morgans was at last beginning to tell, and the protective shield of handicap on which some of the other cars relied could not protect them any longer. By the seventieth lap, Laird, who was consistently lapping at speeds above 90 m.p.h., found himself in third place. Soon after this he handed the sash to Lones who set off at tremendous speed in his 730-c.c. car. By the eightieth lap he was still in third place but, like his predecessors, still gaining on the opposition. When the chequered flag finally fell, Lones had carried the Morgan sash into second place, with an Austin team ahead and a mixed team behind.

Few important alterations were made to Morgans during 1933, but the old two-speed machine was finally dropped. However, in November the entire light-car world raised its eyebrows at the remarkable news of a new four-cylinder Morgan using an 8-h.p. Ford engine. *The Light Car and Cyclecar* had this to say about it: . . . No manufacturer can afford to lag behind in these days of keen competition. The four-cylinder Morgan does not supplant an existing model, it is an addition to the range and a worthy addition which will undoubtedly prove immensely popular with hundreds of people who have wanted a four-cylinder model bearing the name of Morgan and who will welcome the newcomer with open arms.'

While the new car still looked very much like the regular Morgans, it was in fact remarkably different in a number of ways. For the first time it now had what may be called a conventional Z-section chassis, made for Morgans by their present chassis makers: Rubery-Owen Ltd. The hollow tube backbone through which the propeller-shaft ran remained. The brake pedal was for the first time connected to all three wheels, while the handbrake was connected only to the rear wheel. The new chassis was a foot longer than its predecessor, making the wheel-base 8 ft. 3 in. and track 4 ft. 2 in. The engine had modified thermo-siphon cooling, forced lubrication and coil ignition. The car was a four-seater and by Morgan standards really quite roomy. In spite of all these improvements the price remained very reasonable at £120. H.F.S. had, in fact, started experimenting with a four-cylinder Dorman engine and later a Coventry-Climax engine in a Morgan four years before, but had decided not to launch a four-cylinder model until they had found an engine that would give comparable performance to a V-twin. This was a very good time at Malvern, and in April 1934 it was reported that V-twin models were selling like hot cakes, with the demand for four-cylinder models far exceeding the availability of engines.

In July the same Morgan team that had done so well in the 1933 Relay Grand Prix again came second. Again Rhodes took the first stint and Laird the second, and by the time the two-thirds stage of the race had arrived he was in sixth place. Lones now took the sash for the final part but his task was by no means easy, for the sunshine with which the afternoon had begun had now turned to heavy rain. Nevertheless, he steadily forced his way forward and by the eightieth lap it was virtually certain that he would come second. His luck held and the Morgan team happily found themselves runners-up for the second year in succession.

August brought some more good news for Morgans. Clive Lones broke eight records at Brooklands in his 498-c.c. Morgan, including 5 km. at 86.72 m.p.h., 50 miles at 84.23 m.p.h. and two hours at 80.72 m.p.h.

The 1935 models which appeared at the 1934 Motor Cycle Show had few new features. The four-cylinder model and the V-twin Super Sports both had the improved tails introduced in 1933, carrying the spare wheel in a far more elegant way: instead of having it perched horizontally on top of the tail, it was now fitted diagonally at the tip—hence the description 'the cork in the bottle look'. At the Show the price of the V-twin Family model was quoted as £105, yet in February 1935 it was down to £95.

1935 was not a good year for Morgans in terms of competitions, but it was an exciting year as regards the development of the car. Two new Morgan models were announced at the 1935 Motor Cycle Show and the Morgan stand with its nine complete cars and two chassis was a centre of great interest, all the more so because there was only one other three-wheeler stand in the whole show—the B.S.A.

The two new models were both of the four-cylinder type, one being a two-seater with an 8-h.p. Ford engine and the other a two-seater with the 10-h.p. engine as used in the De Luxe Ford. The prices were 115 guineas and 122 guineas respectively, while the original four-seater model F was offered at 110 guineas. The V-twins, too, were still going strong and like the Ford-engined cars were available in three models: Super Sports, Sports Two-Seater, and Family, with prices ranging from the Family model at 92 guineas to the o.h.v. air-cooled Super Sports at 120 guineas. It is interesting to note that J.A.P. engines were no longer available for the V-twins—specially produced Matchless engines were used instead. For many years, H.F.S. had shopped around for engines but no one except J.A.P. had been in a position to produce them in lare enough quantities until now. The new Matchless engine was probably the best of its kind available and as the company was in a position to meet Morgan's reduced demand for V-twins at this time, it is understandable that H.F.S. went over to Matchless. However, it did sadly mean that the long relationship with

J.A.P. which had been so successful for both companies was finally ending.

Although Morgans had produced two new models for the 1935 Show, this was not the full extent of their efforts, for behind the scenes several years of research were nearing fruition in an entirely new project for the company, a project which was fully revealed to the motoring world just before the dawning of 1936.

THE CAR THAT TOUCHED A POLICEMAN
Drawn by H. M. Bateman

Cartoon from The Tatler, *25th November 1927*

The Coming of Four Wheels 1935·1950

Two days after Christmas 1935, *The Light Car and Cyclecar* announced a four-wheeler Morgan. Although this was a great step forward for the company it did not altogether come as a surprise to the motoring world. Indeed, it had been expected for some time and those whose powers of observation were particularly good might have seen H. F. S. Morgan testing out his prototype machine at Brooklands in the summer of 1935. The original article about the 4/4 described the car as follows: 'It has an open two-seater body with luggage space behind the seats and two spare wheels are mounted at the rear. The engine is a four-cylinder Coventry Climax in unit with a Borg and Beck clutch from which a short shaft runs to a four-speed gearbox mounted amidships in the chassis and controlled directly by a delightfully stubby lever. An open Hardy-Spicer prop. shaft completes the transmission to the spiral-bevel back axle. The engine delivers 34 b.h.p. at 4,500 r.p.m.' It further went on to describe how the steering and front suspension remained of the typical Morgan pattern, and commented that: 'the car handles very nicely and is exceptionally lively.' The Climax engine had a capacity of 1,122 c.c. having overhead push-rod-operated inlet valves and side exhaust valves, and it gave the car a top speed of over 70 m.p.h. In February the price was announced and no one could deny that 185 guineas was indeed good value. It was typical of H.F.S. to enter the new car in a trial as soon as it was announced, and so he put his name down for the London to Exeter which was held just

Early advertisement for the 4/4, October 1936

after Christmas 1935. He won a premier award and repeated this success in the London to Land's End trial in April 1936. Thus the car was launched in ideal circumstances. People would have had the confidence to buy it anyway as it carried the Morgan name, but this instant success in trials removed any possible doubt.

The 4/4 had of course missed the 1935 Motor Show and so it was an historic day in 1936 when a Morgan Stand was first seen at the Motor Show (until this time it had, of course, only appeared at the Motor Cycle Show). In some ways this delay was possibly all to the good, as the months between the announcement of the car and its appearance at the Show had given Morgans time to carry out a number of minor but significant improvements. The cooling system was altered to give a considerably lower running temperature, and an air-cooled belt-driven dynamo replaced the old-fashioned chain-driven dynamo and distributor unit. The distributor was of course now quite separate and driven by skew gears from the timing chain. Vibration was reduced by fitting rubber blocks between the engine mountings and the chassis. The front suspension, while remaining basically the same, was also improved and the vertical spindles on which the front wheels slide up and down were increased in diameter from $\frac{3}{4}$ in. to 1 in.

The steering, too, came in for change. The reduction box, which for some years had been mounted on Morgan steering columns, was now dispensed with and replaced by a Burman-Douglas steering box at the bottom of the column. The car was received with very great enthusiasm at the

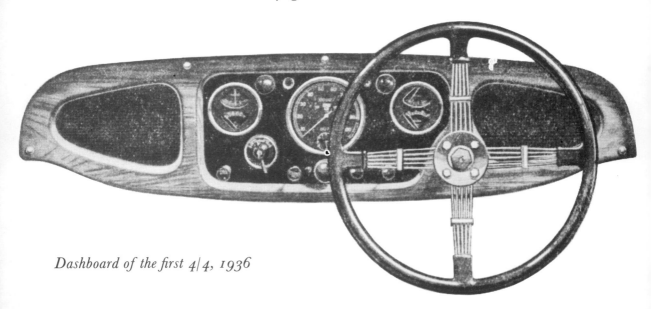

Dashboard of the first 4/4, 1936

Show and its success was quickly assured. But Morgans were very keen to show that the day of the three-wheeler was not over and gone, and so throughout the year little snippets appeared in motoring journals, with comments from H.F.S. to the effect that although the three-wheeler market had become more restricted, it would never die. The proof of his sincerity was revealed at the Motor Cycle Show of 1936 where Morgans still held a stand, although they were the only representatives there of three-wheeler cars. Counting the various alternative engines available, Morgans were offering a total of nine different three-wheelers for 1937, although there were in fact now only three main body designs: Super Sports, Sports and four-seater. Five types of twin-cylinder and four types of four-cylinder machines were listed and prices ranged from £102 to £128.

But two unfortunate events clouded the excellent Morgan year of 1936. Firstly, in October, fire broke out in the body-building shop at the Pickersleigh Road factory and destroyed the greater part of that bay and its contents. However, H.F.S. was able to have the damaged part rebuilt quickly and I understand that the only serious effect of the trouble was to make deliveries run a few weeks late for a period of a few months. The second unfortunate happening was a sad one indeed, for on 10th November George Morgan died at the age of eighty-four. *The Light Car and Cyclecar* headed the obituary 'A Pioneer Passes Away', and paid great tribute to the interest and enthusiasm which he had always displayed in Morgans and in light-car racing.

The 4/4 was received in France with the same enthusiasm that had greeted the three-wheelers after the First World War, when Darmont began to build his French version. Stewart Sandford had been selling three-wheeler Morgans for some time at his Paris showroom, in addition to his own cars, but with the advent of the 4/4 the demand became impossible to meet. Frenchmen found the new Morgan so attractive that Sandford was able to sell on sight and found himself severely restricted by his import quota. When the franc was devalued he decided, in March 1937, to start making 4/4s in his own factory. He therefore imported the chassis in pieces, together with the engines, and assembled them. He produced his own bodies, which were exact replicas of the Morgan body, and a Paris correspondent predicted that before long many of them would be seen in French motor-racing circles.

One of the greatest Morgan achievements of the 1930s was winning its class in the R.A.C. Rally for three consecutive

years, 1937–8–9. George Goodall was the driver on each
occasion, and the first of his successes came in March 1937.
In May the Edinburgh trial brought proof that the emphasis
in competitions had swung away from three-wheelers
towards four-wheelers. No less than seven 4/4s competed in
the trial—among them Peter Morgan driving in a competition for the first time, and his father. They both won silver
medals although four of the other four-wheelers won
premier awards. Only two three-wheelers were entered and
their results were not outstanding. In August yet another
indication of the change of emphasis came when a four-
seater version of the 4/4 was announced at a cost of £235.

In the three-wheeler department, the major development
for the 1937 Motor Cycle Show was the Super Sports in
four-cylinder form, although the o.h.v. air-cooled Matchless
Super Sports was still available.

In spite of all these developments at the works, H.F.S. was
by 1937 giving considerably less of his time to the Company.
By this time he had established his home at Bray in Berkshire
and although he visited Malvern every week he was not any
longer able to give full-time personal attention. It was not
that he cared any the less, it was simply that for personal

The first 4/4 four-seater, 1937

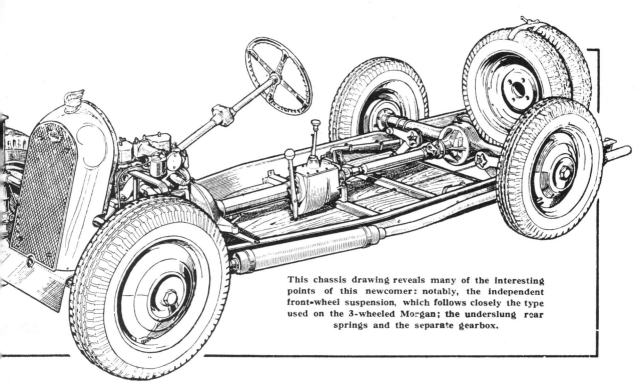

This chassis drawing reveals many of the interesting points of this newcomer: notably, the independent front-wheel suspension, which follows closely the type used on the 3-wheeled Morgan; the underslung rear springs and the separate gearbox.

The 4/4 chassis, 1936

reasons he had decided to change the pattern of his life. He therefore appointed his excellent works manager, George Goodall, to the post of managing director late in 1937 and took on the post of chairman which had been left vacant by George Morgan's death in November 1936.

1938 produced another enormous entry in the Land's End trial held in April: a total of ten four-wheelers and seven three-wheelers, with the Morgans, father and son, and the Goodalls, father and son, among the drivers in the former category. A total of five premier awards was won by the seventeen drivers, so the result was not outstanding.

Far more impressive was George Goodall's triumph in May, when he won the class for open touring cars up to 10 h.p. in the R.A.C. Rally for the second time. *The Light Car and Cyclecar* said: 'Some people believe that winning big prizes in an affair like the R.A.C. Rally is just sheer luck. Well, as the aristocrats of the screen would say, take a load of this. George Goodall's win is not luck: it is thoroughness, skill, a good car and experience. It wouldn't surprise me if he won the class next year.' How prophetic these words turned out to be!

In the next month, a brave young lady called Miss Fawcett assisted by Mr. White entered a 4/4 in the Le Mans 24-hour race with considerable success. Of the forty-two starters she came in thirteenth, although her 1,098-c.c. car had been up against opposition machines of as much as 4.5 litres. Unfortunately she did not win her class—that prize was captured by a Singer which came in eighth—but it was nevertheless something to be proud of and it was not until the 1960s that Morgans improved on her attempt.

A further example of Morgan's ever-increasing swing to four wheels was the creation of the luxurious drophead coupé model, announced in October 1938. It was available as a two-seater at £236, and in order that the total number of models produced at Malvern should not be too excessive the F 2 three-wheeler tourer was dropped. Otherwise, the twin- and four-cylinder engined three-wheelers continued right up to the war, with no change in design.

February 1939 saw the introduction of the last new Morgan introduced before the war—the Le Mans replica. It cost £250 and had a top speed of fully 80 m.p.h. Its distinguishing features were its cycle-type front wings, folding windscreen, fly screen and single spare wheel. The engine capacity was 24 c.c. smaller than that of the other 4/4s, but the cylinder head, valves and parts were all carefully polished and the crankshaft was precision balanced.

The 4/4 drophead coupé, 1938

In May 1939 came the announcement of a new engine for the 4/4s, specially produced by Standard Motor Co. This unit, which had all overhead valves and a capacity of 1,267 c.c., at once became standard on the coupé and available as an optional extra on other 4/4s at a cost of £5. The new engine gave 38.8 b.h.p. at 4,800 r.p.m. and could be run at speeds up to 5,500 r.p.m. The engine was provided with a Solex downdraught carburettor, and much more rubber was used in the mounting so that the car ran extra smoothly.

The other important event in May was George Goodall's third consecutive class win in the R.A.C. Rally, which neatly fulfilled *The Light Car* prophecy. But the 1939 Rally was the best of all for Morgans because in addition to Goodall's success, H.F.S. and Peter Morgan jointly won the Light Car Trophy and a 'handsome electric clock' for coming first in the class for closed cars up to 10 h.p. They were driving a drophead coupé with the hood up.

The double success in the R.A.C. Rally was the last important Morgan win before the war and a wonderful note to end on. Petrol rationing was introduced only a few weeks after the Rally, hitting three-wheeler users very seriously since they received a disproportionately small allowance. This was later adjusted but by that time the Morgan factory had closed for the war.

As the war years are accounted for in 'The Business History' I will not take up space on them here, except to point out that all production of Morgans and all competitions ceased during this period.

The story begins again in March 1945 when, with the end of the war for the first time beginning to come in sight, Mr. and Mrs. Morgan gave a large party at the Winter Gardens in Malvern for three hundred of the employees and friends of the firm. Then, towards the end of the year, work began on assembling a few cars from spare parts.

1946 was, as I have said in 'The Business History', largely taken up with preparing the factory for going back into production and a few more cars were assembled out of spares, most of them being exported to Australia. More important than this, however, were the improvements carried out on the 4/4. As the new Standard engine was only announced in May 1939, it had been incorporated in very few of the cars built before the war. Thus, as far as the general public was concerned, this was a new feature. The front suspension, too, had changed since pre-war days. Although the same basic design was still in use it now had a simple form of steering damper fitted, which very effectively eliminated the traditional Morgan wheel-wobble.

The three-wheeler models remained unchanged, and Morgan was certainly the first firm to start producing three-wheelers after the war. The four-seater model had an 8-h.p. Ford engine and the F-Super had a similar unit of 10 h.p. Production of these continued until 1951, the last one leaving the factory early in 1952. The price list at this time was as follows:

4/4 Drophead Coupé	£435 + £121 purchase tax
4/4 Four-seater	£408 + £114 purchase tax
4/4 Two-seater	£390 + £109 purchase tax
F4 Four-seater	£235 + £66 purchase tax
F Super	£260 + £73 purchase tax

The F4, 1947

The F Super, 1947

As petrol rationing was still very severe in the early post-war years, no competitions were held in the period 1946–8 but at last, by the end of 1948, the rationing restrictions had been sufficiently eased to enable a miniature Exeter run to take place on New Year's Day 1949—for the first time in ten years. The run was only 56 miles long and the weather conditions were appalling. Nevertheless, about half the cars entered came through without losing marks. Unfortunately it was not a very spectacular re-entry into the competition world for Morgans, as only W. A. Goodall secured a first-class award. Peter Morgan and C. J. McCann did, however, at least succeed in gaining second-class awards. Any disappointment felt at this event must have been fully compensated for by Morgan's success in the first post-war Land's End trial which was held, like the Exeter, in a 'mini' form at Easter 1949. Five Morgans were entered in the 52-mile run round the roads and hills of Devonshire, and the one-make team award was won by the Morgans driven by Peter Morgan, W. A. Goodall and C. J. McCann. Another Morgan driven by R. Hillier also won a premier award.

Apart from these events 1949 was not a specially significant year in the Morgan world, and nor was 1950 until the announcement of a new car: the Morgan Plus-4, powered by a 2,088-c.c. Standard Vanguard engine. The car was announced in *The Autocar* in September and replaced the 4/4 in all its forms. The Vanguard engine developed 68 b.h.p. at 4,300 r.p.m. and was o.h.v. with push-rods. One of the new features on the car was that for the first time the front suspension could be lubricated with engine oil under pressure at the touch of a button. The new car, being faster, used larger tyres than the 4/4 (5.25 × 16) and was available in all three body styles previously featured on the 4/4. It was also a little more roomy, since the width across the seat had been increased by 2 in. and the leg-room by a similar amount. The bonnet was a little longer than previously and the radiator slightly higher. The prices, too, were a little higher, as the two-seater model cost £625 including purchase tax and the drophead coupé £723.

In the best Morgan tradition, the Plus-4 won its spurs almost immediately through its competition successes.

The Fifties and Sixties

At last, by late 1950, England was well enough on the way towards complete recovery from the war to be able to resume motor racing and motor trials, without having to worry about keeping distances as short as possible in order to save petrol. The fifties and sixties are a most interesting period in Morgan history as it was during this time that people first began to think of the Morgan as being 'old-fashioned', although it proved itself to be more than a match for its rivals, time after time.

The racing and competition successes during this period seem to have come in phases: the early 1950s were on the whole unspectacular, while the period 1958–66 was outstanding. A further somewhat barren period followed this, yet, by the beginning of the 1970s, it became clear that the Morgan's day in trials and competitions was by no means done.

Probably the most significant event in 1950 was one which came at the very end of the year: the London to Exeter trial.

Peter Morgan and Archie Weave in the 1950 London to Exeter trial

It was the first time for twelve years that this event had taken place in its full pre-war form, and it was here that the newly launched Plus-4 won its spurs by gaining a premier award. A total entry of 256 was received of which 169 were four-wheeler cars, 4 were three-wheelers and 69 were motor-cycles. Conditions were particularly bad that year and so it was very satisfactory that, in addition to Peter Morgan's premier award in the Plus-4, C. J. McCann should also have gained one in his 4/4.

Of the four three-wheeler entries in the trial, three were of course, Morgans, although they did not fare so well—only one succeeded in winning a second, while the other two were not listed.

In 1951 the R.A.C. organized their first International Rally of Great Britain and a number of Morgans enthusiastically joined the 226 starters. The rally was one of the first post-war events seriously comparable with the old A.C.U. Six-Day Trials, in that it was a real test of driving skill and of the stamina of normal production motor cars. The event included a speed test at Silverstone and an extremely long drive, taking several days to travel through England, Wales and Scotland and then back to Bournemouth in time for a great rally banquet. In the old tradition there were specially timed hill sections, an extremely tricky speed test on a 1.9-mile road circuit in Wales, which included plenty of extremely difficult corners and switchbacks, and some very nasty narrow and badly surfaced roads in Scotland. It was a great triumph for the Morgan team, consisting of Peter Morgan, W. A. G. Goodall and Dr. Steel, to win the team prize as competition was very fierce. In fact, in the final result Peter Morgan and W. A. G. Goodall came second and third overall. As *Autosport* said: 'These grand little cars did remarkably well to take second and third place in the open class from the largest number of XK 120 Jaguars ever to assemble for a competitive event.' As a matter of interest, no less than 37 of these Jaguars were in the entry list.

But this rally success was by no means a flash in the pan, for in April 1952 the same drivers once again won the team prize—and this in direct competition with 24 other one-make teams. The rally was organized in very much the same way as in the previous year, except that a light fall of sleet at Silverstone caused the first speed test to be cancelled, to the great disgust of the competitors. The Morgan team did consistently well throughout, and when the final results were published Peter Reece was placed fifth and Peter Morgan sixth in the open class.

Private owners' team in the 1952 R.A.C. Rally—Bancroft, Ray and Reece

Another Morgan team composed of Bancroft (who had done very well in his Plus-4 in the 1952 R.A.C. Rally), Reece and Ray came close to winning the Morecambe National Jubilee Rally in May. This would have been a magnificent achievement, with a total field of 300 entries, but unfortunately the Morecambe system of points meant that if a single mark was lost a competitor was sunk and, in fact, only 110 people did manage to get through without losing marks. The Morgan team was leading when, unfortunately, Ray dropped one mark in the final tests and put it out of the running. However, Morgan honour was fully redeemed by Ken Bancroft being declared the outright winner.

Apart from these events there is only one other important milestone of Morgan history to be found in 1952, and it is a rather sad one: in February the last three-wheeler ever to leave the factory was collected by its owner. An era and, indeed, a great era had ended—but H.F.S. had a good reason for stopping three-wheeler production as you will read in 'The Business History'.

Little of great interest happened in 1953, except that at the end of the year the present style of the car was adopted for all models—the chrome headlamps were done away with and replaced by lamps flared into the front wings and, at the same time, the vertical radiator grille was replaced by the curved one of today. This was the only time between 1935 and the present day that Morgans have undergone a major change of styling. It was done in an attempt to keep up with the times, but one person was not too happy about it—Peter

*The Plus-4 two-seater, 1950–53 (above), and the
Plus-4 four-seater after the restyling of 1953 (below)*

THE MORGAN PLUS FOUR 4 SEATER

The Outstanding Four Seater Sports Car for 1963

Morgan said at the time that he was sure the new design would have to be superseded within five years. That was almost twenty years ago, and there is no sign of any new style yet, thank goodness!

From its inception the Plus-4 was well received and a very successful car. But there was one problem: there was always a shortage of Standard Vanguard engines to power it. After it became known than an improved version of this engine, to power the Triumph TR2, was coming out, and that only about five of these per week would be made available to Morgans, H.F.S. decided to reintroduce the 4/4 in time for the 1955 Motor Show. This was the Series II, powered by a 10-h.p. side-valve Ford engine. The new 4/4 was described as a tourer only—it was not meant to be a true sports car like the Plus-4—but it did at least bring sporting motoring of a sort within the range of some enthusiasts with limited resources. Its price was £713 as against over £820 for the Plus-4, but then its 0–60 m.p.h. time of 29.6 seconds was no match for the Plus-4's 10.8 seconds. The Plus-4 began to be fitted with the TR 2 engine early in 1954, and then adopted the TR 3 engine when it came out in 1956.

The Plus-4 drophead coupé, 1954

On the sporting side neither 1956 nor 1957 were exciting years, although J. T. Spare had one great success in his Morgan: he won his class in the 1956 R.A.C. Rally and came in third overall. Only an Aston Martin and a Jaguar were able to get the better of him. When one comes to 1958, however, things were very different: it was in that year that the great post-war period of Morgan racing successes began, when a young racing driver who had been competing on a shoestring for about eight years decided to have one more fling—if it succeeded he would go on, but if it failed he would give up racing for ever. His final fling consisted of putting up all his savings, together with those of his fiancée, and buying a 1956 Morgan Plus-4. The man I am referring to is Chris Lawrence. Although he had not at that time started his tuning business (he was then working in the aircraft industry), he was a competent amateur engine-tuner and so well set up to work on his Morgan. At that time the best form of racing in which a relatively unknown driver could make his name was marque racing, which has since come to be called 'Mod Sports' racing. At that time marque racing existed for certain specified types of car only, including Triumph TR4, Morgan Plus-4, A.C. Ace, Austin-Healey and M.G.A. A whole season of races for these cars was arranged annually, and competitors stood to win the B.A.R.C. Freddie Dixon Trophy.

On the face of it Lawrence's first race, which was held at Aintree, was not a success, for he was placed last. However, it was one of those races where only a few hundred yards separated the first and last car and so he felt sufficiently encouraged to press on. Sure enough, by the end of the 1958 season he held the lap record for marque racing and was in a position to enter the 1959 season with renewed confidence.

1958 also brought the first of three Morgan successes in the annual Six-Hour Relay Race at Silverstone. This was the longest British race at the time—some commentators used to compare it to Le Mans, although it only lasted one-quarter as long. Each team entering the relay race was given a sash and was required to have only one car in the race at any one time. No laps covered by a car which was not carrying its team's sash counted in the total.

The Morgan Plus-4 team consisted of Morgan, Meredith, Mayman and Belcher, and found itself competing against twenty other teams. The race began at 1 o'clock with a Le Mans-style start, and thus what was destined to be a singularly frustrating event for the Morgans got under way.

By 3 o'clock it was noticed with considerable surprise that

one of the hotted-up Austin A.35s of the Speedwell Stable (whose drivers included John Sprinzel and Graham Hill) had, thanks to its 32-lap handicap, shot from sixth place to equal second during the previous half-hour. By the half-time mark at 4 o'clock it was in the lead, with the Morgan Plus-4 half a lap behind in second place. It was fast becoming clear that the race would hereafter revolve around a ding-dong battle between these two teams—and so it did. The Morgan put on a spurt and by 4.30 had drawn level with the Speedwell car. Thirty minutes later the Morgan had a lead of 0.7 of a lap—125 laps against the Speedwell's 124.3. Now it was the turn of the Speedwell team to put on a spurt, which it did with great effect under the urgent direction of the team manager, Mason. Sadly, by 6 o'clock Morgan was back in second place. It is possible that the Morgan might have reversed the situation by the end of the race, but, unfortunately, much valuable time was lost at about 6.30. It was then that Meredith went out to do the final stint and was obliged to come into the pits after only one lap with a loose bonnet. Precious minutes were lost trying to mend it before he went out again, only to return one lap later and hand the sash on to Mayman.

In spite of all the wasted time, Mayman succeeded through some very hard driving in cutting the Speedwell lead down to only 0.3 of a lap by the time the chequered flag fell.

In 1959 Lawrence entered all 22 races for the Freddie Dixon Trophy and, unbelievably, won 21 of them, coming third in the remaining one. As a result, he won the trophy by an overwhelming majority. In that year he also branched out into sports car racing in the 1,600–2,600-c.c. class, entering, amongst others, the Autosport August Bank Holiday meeting at Goodwood. His Morgan led for 19 of the 21 laps, and he finished a close second to a Jaguar.

In the same month a Morgan team, including Lawrence, put up another outstanding performance in the Six-Hour Relay Race at Silverstone. Apart from numerous club teams, the one-make teams comprised Jaguar (C- and D-types), Jaguar XKs, Fairthorpe Electron, Lotus, T.V.R., Triumph TR, M.G., Austin-Healey and Morgan.

The race began at 1 o'clock. Although Lawrence's Morgan was the first car to get under way, a D-type Jaguar was ahead of him by the end of the first lap. After one hour's racing the Morgan team's morale was dropping, as they found themselves fourth behind the Fairthorpe Electrons, the M.G.A.s and the Healey Sprites. But the Morgan men really meant business and *Autosport* reported that their team manager was taking matters very seriously. By 2.30 the situation had changed considerably, and the Morgans found themselves third after the Lotuses and the Electrons. Half an hour later these pushy Morgans had succeeded in grasping second place with 95.7 laps, while the leaders—the Electrons —had now clocked up 97.3. At 3.30, with less than half the race run, the Morgans had fallen back a little further behind the Electrons, although these two makes still held first and second places, but by the time the half-way mark was reached they were only one lap behind. They were on the way up now and, sure enough, within half an hour they were in the lead, with the Electrons behind them being closely pursued by the TRs who by 5 o'clock had come up to second place and were only one lap behind the Morgans. The TRs were now really after the Morgans and the Morgans knew it well—it made them all the more determined. In fact, the TRs did, for a while, lose second place to the Octagon Stable's team of twin-cam M.G.s. But by 6 o'clock—with one hour to go—the Morgans had the TRs back in second place, and a quarter of an hour later the leading TR was shown to be only 45 seconds behind Lawrence. It was clear that an exciting finish was on the way, especially when it was reported at 6.25 that Hurrell in the leading TR was gaining on Lawrence at the rate of two seconds per lap. Then Lawrence had some bad luck: a D-type spun at Woodcote just in front of him, forcing him to slacken his speed, and soon after 6.30 only 19 seconds separated the TRs from the Morgans. By 6.45 yet another second had been taken off the Morgan lead. Lawrence and Hurrell were going absolutely flat out now, and after a few more minutes of magnificent driving the flag fell and the Morgan team were the declared winners by 19 seconds.

One of the minor side-effects of Lawrence's successes in 1958 and 1959 was to make a deep impression on Peter Morgan. It was not only his ability to drive the car well that Morgan admired, but also his ability to get extra performance out of it by skilful tuning. Morgan therefore arranged with Lawrence that he would prepare a certain number of TR 3 engines for him every month. This was how a new model was added to the Morgan range in 1960—the Plus-4 Super Sports. One must remember that this was before the days of the Mini-Cooper and the Lotus-Cortina, and so it was an unusually forward-looking step for Morgan to take. Nowadays we are all used to manufacturers fitting their cars with engines prepared by outside specialists, but in

The Plus-4 Super Sports, 1960

1960 Morgan was the only one. The Super Sports was basically a Plus-4 two-seater fitted with wire wheels as standard and an aluminium alloy lightweight body. The Lawrencetune engine was fitted with a fully balanced crankshaft and flywheel, and the pistons and connecting rods were prepared with similar care. Other modifications included a fully polished and gas-flowed cylinder head, an oil cooler, a special camshaft, twin Weber carburettors and a four-branch exhaust system. The car was considerably more lively than the Plus-4, and as opposed to the latter's top speed of 105 m.p.h., most Super Sports models could reach the 120 m.p.h. mark. Production of this model continued until shortly before the advent of the Plus-8.

Before we leave the 1950s behind us entirely, there is one sad event that cannot be passed over—the death of H.F.S., which occurred in June 1959. Although he was less directly involved with the company in his last years, his enthusiasm for Morgans and his interest in the company never diminished. Peter Morgan was especially sad that his father did not live to witness the fiftieth anniversary celebrations which were held in April 1960.

To celebrate the company's Golden Jubilee, Peter Morgan arranged a banquet lunch at the Abbey Hotel in Malvern. The guests included the senior staff at the works, representatives of all the companies who had supplied components over the years, representatives of the main Morgan agents, and some of the great Morgan drivers of early days such as W. G. McMinnies. It was an occasion that will be remembered by all who were fortunate enough to be present and it was a great milestone in the company's history.

To return to racing: 1960 saw Chris Lawrence entering a number of foreign events. Although he was going to drive a Lola, he decided to take his Morgan abroad too. He used it to get to know circuits like Nurburgring and Spa and was immensely impressed by its performance, although he did not race it abroad that year. At home he moved out of marque racing and into proper sports car racing. He came third in the Whitsun meeting at Goodwood, even though the opposition included D-type Jaguars and Porsches, and in the autumn won a sports car race at Oulton Park.

1960, although unspectacular, served to convince Lawrence more fully than ever that Morgans were ideal for him, and so, early in 1961, he bought a new Plus-4 Super Sports and took it off to Nurburgring where he entered it in the 1,000-km. race. Although he did not finish the race he astonished everyone, especially the Germans, by breaking the Porsche-held 2-litre lap record quite substantially. Indeed, he reduced the time from 10.38 to 10.31. The organizers of the meeting were so staggered that his curious machine, 'which only seemed to spend a quarter of the race on the ground', could travel so fast that they presented him with a special award.

Other successes swiftly followed: soon after the Nurburgring event Lawrence's team-mate, Richard Shepherd-Barron, entered a Morgan in the Grand Prix de Spa in Belgium and finished this three-hour race second overall. Elated by their successes, Lawrence and Shepherd-Barron moved on to Le Mans, but here their luck was out. The scrutineers took one glance at the Morgan and decided that it must be a 1939 car that had been resprayed and fitted with disc brakes. In view of this, they refused to allow it to compete in the 24-hour race. Although the authorities at Spa confirmed that it was a fast and excellent car, the scrutineers at Le Mans were unmoved, and so the two men went on to Monza where Lawrence finished second, sandwiched between two Porsches in the Coppa Inter-Europa. It was in this race that he carried out one of his cleverest ploys. As the Morgan he was driving had been built for Le Mans, he knew that he was in no danger of running out of petrol. Nevertheless, throughout the practice he kept on coming into the pits to take on fuel. The Porsche team noticed this and accordingly were not worried when after two and a half hours of racing Lawrence was in the lead—they were expecting him to stop and refuel at any moment. Then, with only fifteen minutes' racing to go, they realized that the Morgan was *not* going to stop and, although they put on all possible pressure, only one Porsche had succeeded in overtaking the Morgan by the end of the race.

The 1962 season saw a Morgan finish in second place again in the Grand Prix de Spa. After the race Lawrence and Shepherd-Barron went back to Le Mans, which was a good effort considering that they had in effect been snubbed in the previous year. This time all was well, and the car received the unconditional approval of the scrutineers. The two men were greatly relieved and set to work to plan the race in detail. They decided that Lawrence would be less bothered by the tricky light conditions at dusk and at dawn, and so the race timetable was drawn up as follows:

Saturday	4.00 p.m.– 7.00 p.m.	Lawrence
Saturday	7.00 p.m.–10.00 p.m.	Shepherd-Barron
Saturday/		
Sunday	10.00 p.m.– 1.00 a.m.	Lawrence
Sunday	1.00 a.m.– 4.00 a.m.	Shepherd-Barron
Sunday	4.00 a.m.– 7.00 a.m.	Lawrence
Sunday	7.00 a.m.–10.00 a.m.	Shepherd-Barron
Sunday	10.00 a.m.– 1.00 p.m.	Lawrence
Sunday	1.00 p.m.– 4.00 p.m.	Shepherd-Barron

The Morgan's petrol tank held almost enough fuel for four hours' running, so that there was never any danger of running out of fuel towards the end of one of the three-hour stints. The only thing which had Lawrence a little worried was his racing camshaft. He only guaranteed this for 2,000 racing miles and, as it turned out, the car covered no less than 2,256 miles in the race. Happily, it gave no trouble and although a competent pit staff, including Jim Goodall and Charlie Curtis from the Morgan works, were at hand, they were never required to do more than fill the car up with petrol and oil.

Chris Lawrence with his Le Mans engine

Richard Shepherd-Barron winning his class at Le Mans, 1962

The car never made an unscheduled pit-stop at any time in the race and even when, with four hours to go, the exhaust pipe broke close to the manifold, Lawrence pressed on. At the next scheduled stop a brief attempt was made to mend it but they were anxious to waste as little time as possible. Apart from the appalling noise, the broken exhaust really mattered very little though it may have cost them a couple of hundred revs. on the straight.

During one of his rest periods on the Saturday evening, Lawrence saw Peter Morgan standing by the Morgan pit looking wistfully up the track. 'It will be nice to see the old car coming up there at 4 o'clock on Sunday, won't it?' said Lawrence. This was exactly how it happened. At 4 o'clock on Sunday the two men, standing side by side, watched Shepherd-Barron take the chequered flag for the 2-litre G.T. class—possibly the greatest Morgan success since the 1913 Grand Prix at Amiens. The car, whose average speed for the race was 94 m.p.h., had at times lapped as fast as 110 m.p.h., very nearly hitting 130 m.p.h. on the straight. Both drivers had been determined not to push it too hard, and although they were tempted to try to catch up with the Rover gas-turbine car which was not all that far ahead, they wisely refrained from getting carried away by their enthusiasm.

Lawrence and his Morgan also did well at home in 1962 for, in addition to coming second overall in the Autosport Championship, he could claim by the end of the year to hold the lap record for the 1,600–2,000-c.c. class at every major British circuit. Most of these records stood for about four years.

But the Morgan competition successes in 1962 were not confined to Lawrence and Shepherd-Barron: using Lawrence's car, Adrian Dence brought about the second Morgan victory in the Freddie Dixon Trophy for marque racing.

The Morgan 4/4 Club (now called the Morgan Sports Car Club) was also highly successful in 1962. Its most spectacular triumph was in the Six-Hour Relay Race in which its team came second. The drivers were Ray Meredith, Brian Redman, Bob Duggan and Chris Pickard in Plus-4s, and John McKechnie in a 4/4.

In spite of a rather slow Le Mans-style start made by Meredith, the Morgan team was lying third after the Jaguar B and A teams when one hour's racing had been completed. During this time Meredith had more than made up for his slow start, indeed he was the star of the 4/4 team and was travelling deceptively fast. When one and a half hours had passed, Meredith came in for a rest and John McKechnie set off in his five-speed 997-c.c. Morgan. Evidently, he kept up very well, in spite of his smaller capacity, for at 3 o'clock the Morgans were still in third place, two laps behind the leading Jaguar B team. A little later Pickard's Morgan began to suffer from dynamo trouble, so Redman took over from him, actually losing very little time. By the half-way mark the Morgan team had come up into second place behind the Jaguar B team and there they remained, gradually nibbling away at the Jaguar lead. By 5 o'clock both the Jaguar B team and the Morgans had covered 198 laps, while the nearest competitors, the Jaguar A team, had completed only 195.7. Bob Duggan was heading the Morgans at this stage, but he was just a fraction slower than his best because he was using rain tyres and the much-expected rain had never come. Soon after 5 o'clock he changed places with Ray Meredith, who immediately began to hot up the pace—so much so, in fact, that his car was gaining six seconds per lap on handicap. Thus by 6 o'clock, with one hour to go, although the Jaguar B team was still leading, the Morgans were only half a lap behind. Everyone was now wondering whether the next hour would give Morgans the chance they needed. Then, luck went against Meredith—the under-tray on his Morgan began to come adrift, forcing him to hand over to Chris Pickard who was just not quite so fast. Any final hope of a Morgan victory was dashed when the one B team Jaguar which was lagging behind was called in, and Wrottesley in a Lister Jaguar was sent out in his place. He soon succeeded in making up the lost time and when the flag fell at 7 o'clock the Jaguar B team had won from the Morgan 4/4 Club by about one minute. It must have been disappointing for the Morganists but, nevertheless, it was a fine result.

1963 brought yet another highly successful racing season for Morgans. Lawrence came second in the Goodwood Tourist Trophy and then with his team-mates, Bill Blydenstein and Pip Arnold, went to Spa where the three Morganists finished first, second and third in the 2,000–2,600-c.c. class. This was quite an unusual team, for although it entered under the name 'Lawrencetune', in fact Chris Lawrence only owned his one car. Blydenstein drove a works machine and Arnold was a private owner. Nevertheless, the team's abilities were even more fully proven when they repeated their 1–2–3 class win at Nurburgring only a week or two after the success at Spa.

1963 brought honours from afar for Morgans, and it was

in South America that one of the most remarkable successes was achieved in 'El Gran Premio National de Automovilismo de Panama'. Only one Morgan was entered and that was a Lawrencetune Super Sports model driven by Pat Kennett, the service manager of the Panamanian agents for Morgan, Triumph and Jaguar.

The race, whose length was 100 miles, was held at a circuit about 50 miles west of Panama city. *Autosport* described the track as follows: 'This airfield circuit is not quite like say, Silverstone or Snetterton. The road hugs the wide runway for 400 yards then swings right at 45° to the other side of the runway then swings left again . . . forming a giant chicane about half a mile long . . . this is followed by a 15-m.p.h. hairpin which takes off the strip on to the service road through the jungle. This is somewhat narrow and stony but dead straight for three-quarters of a mile terminating in a fast right-hander with a bump in the middle.'

Those who doubt that the going was rough should remember that the front end of the Morgan had to be covered with foam rubber to protect it from flying stones. The opposition in the race came from a TR 4 and an E-type Jaguar provided by the Morgan agents, the latter being driven by the head of I.B.M. in Panama, and a Healey 3,000 driven by the Panamanian champion, Ramirez. Beyond these there were two TR3As, a Porsche and a few others (including a second Healey) that do not seem to have been listed anywhere. In the best South American tradition the race began an hour late, but the public's patience was well rewarded by the spectacular Le Mans-style start. The Morgan was soon past the Porsche and the Healey, although overtaking the former obliged Kennett to put at least two wheels on the grass, and soon only the Jaguar lay in front. Kennett used the Jaguar's slip stream to gain a gentle tow in the fastest sections, and in spite of the conditions the two cars were often travelling at speeds in the 120s for the next ten laps. At the chicane a crowd of five thousand cheered with enormous enthusiasm and deftly dodged the shower of stones thrown up to an astonishing height each time the cars passed. It was a burning hot afternoon and the heat soon began to affect some of the cars, causing one of the Healeys to boil. On the eleventh lap the Porsche lost its oil pressure and had to retire, and the E-type's brakes were clearly not enjoying themselves so that Mr. I.B.M. just had to slacken his speed a little. The Morgan saw its chance and in the twelfth lap, in spite of the fact that Kennett felt shot-blasted and was absolutely covered in dirt, swept into the lead.

By the time the three-quarter stage was reached, the order was: Morgan, Healey, Jaguar and TR 4—and then the TR 4 lost its tailpipe. The pits reported that it was not repairable and so he set off again, making the most remarkable noises. Smolen in the E-type became increasingly worried about his brakes and decided to make a pit-stop to see what was wrong. All that resulted from this was that the car caught fire. When it had been extinguished, he had to drive off with his anchors still in their unreliable state.

At about this time another hazard struck—thirst! It was so amazingly hot that Smolen and Homes (in the TR 4) had to stop for refreshment. The Morgan, happily, was fitted with a drinking bottle so this grave problem never troubled Kennett. There was some anxiety on the forty-seventh lap when the Morgan started slowing down: this was understandable, for some weird sounds were coming from the direction of its rear wheels. Ramirez in his Healey was not far behind, but was unable to take advantage of the Morgan's

The winning Morgan in the Panamanian Grand Prix of 1963

slower speed because his front dampers had softened up and were giving him quite a lot of worry on the bumpy bits. With rare skill Kennett managed to keep his rear axle in one piece long enough to finish the race, coming in 39 seconds ahead of Ramirez.

Perhaps the most amazing feature of this race was the condition of the cars at the end of it. The winning Morgan had no rear wheel bearings left at all; Ramirez's Healey, which had come second, had no front suspension left and its tyres were as smooth as the proverbial baby's bottom; the E-type finished on only three tyres with next to no brakes, and the TR 4 with its broken exhaust system was by far the healthiest car left. The only other car to finish was Cortizo in his TR 3 and that wasn't in the best of health. If the race had been ten miles longer one wonders if there would have been any finishers at all! The average speed of the race was 76.9 m.p.h. and the Jaguar and Morgan both completed the equal fastest lap at 81.1 m.p.h. The Morgan had profoundly impressed the crowd and, as *Autosport* pointed out, the last Morgan that had come to Panama had made his mark too—Henry Morgan the pirate.

In 1964 Chris Lawrence teamed up with John Sprinzel and formed the S.L.R. team (Sprinzel Lawrence Racing), for which Lawrence proceeded to build four very special cars. Three of these were based on Morgans and one on a Triumph. The S.L.R. Morgans had beautifully aero-dynamic bodies, and thus it was not entirely surprising that Lawrence was able to reduce his previous Goodwood lap record from 1.42 to 1.39. Later in the year he took his S.L.R. to Spa, where he succeeded in finishing third in his class with two 904 Porsches in front and four behind. The prospects seemed excellent, but unfortunately, while driving back to England, Lawrence had a serious accident (not in a Morgan) which put him out of racing for several months.

In 1965, when he had recovered, Lawrence entered his S.L.R. Morgan in the Brands Hatch Double Five Hundred, which has since become the B.O.A.C. Five Hundred. The car went so well that, although he was on the seventh row of the starting grid, he had a seven-second lead by the end of the first lap. Considering that the opposition included works-prepared E-types and Austin-Healeys, this was a fine performance. The S.L.R. Morgan led the race for 72 laps until a front chassis tube broke. Any normal car would have been put out of the race by this, but not the Morgan. In the pits a box spanner was inserted in the broken chassis tube and bolts were drilled through to hold it in place. Several

Chris Lawrence's S.L.R. Morgan in the 1965 Double Five-Hundred

minutes were lost, but at least Lawrence was able to finish the day's racing. That evening the repair was made more permanent and Lawrence was able to lead for the whole of the second day.

1966 was the last of the great post-war years of racing successes. During that season, Chris Lawrence with his S.L.R. Morgan and Gordon Miles with a Plus-4 Super Sports had numerous successes at Silverstone, Goodwood, Aintree and Castle Combe. It was also during that season that Lawrence set up the marque lap record at Goodwood that holds to this day, and will hold in perpetuity now that Goodwood, alas, is no more.

A little more than half-way through the season, Lawrence had a first-lap accident which wrote off his S.L.R. Morgan and in effect marked the end of a great eight-year period of Morgan victories.

Having now taken a good look at what was happening to
Morgans in the racing world in the early 1960s, let us return
to Malvern Link and see how the car was progressing during
this period. The 4/4 was steadily produced with its 10-h.p.
side-valve engine from 1955 to 1960 when, as a slight con-
cession to modernity, an o.h.v. Ford engine called the 105 E,
with a capacity of 996 c.c. was introduced. This model,
known as the 4/4 Series III, was only in production for about
a year, for at the 1961 Motor Show the Series IV appeared
on the scene with a 1,340-c.c. Ford engine. This made quite a
substantial difference to the car's performance, for while the
weight remained the same, the power was increased from
39 b.h.p. to 54 b.h.p. To help stop this hotter car more
easily, disc brakes were now made standard on the front of
all 4/4 models, and had in fact already been made standard
for Plus-4 models in the previous year.

Peter Morgan's daughter, Lady Jane Colwyn, with the Plus-4-Plus

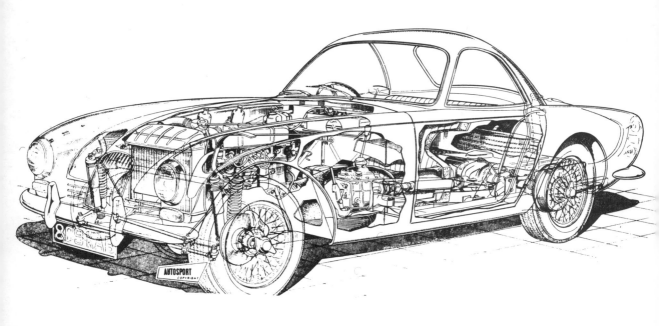

Cutaway drawing of the Plus-4-Plus

But the boldest step Morgans ever took in car design was bringing out the Plus-4-Plus, which appeared at the 1963 Motor Show. In general it was well received, and certainly it was a great surprise to the whole motoring world to find Morgans bringing out such a modern-looking car. The Plus-4-Plus was almost identical in every respect except outward appearance to the ordinary Plus-4. It had the same engine, chassis and suspension but, unlike any other Morgan before or since, it had a lockable boot. Its price at £1,275 made it the most expensive Morgan ever produced at that time. As regards performance and roadholding, the Plus-4-Plus was every bit as good as the normal Plus-4, nor was the price as high as all that. Nevertheless, only fifty were ever made and it seems a miracle that the company did not lose money on the venture.

Also, in 1964, the power of the 4/4 was increased yet again by fitting a 1,500-c.c. Ford engine in what now became the Series V. This engine, as *The Small Car* of August 1964 said, finally removed the feeling that the 4/4 was a poor relation of the Plus-4. It now became a real sports car in its own right and in its competition form, when fitted with a special cylinder-head and camshaft, dual-choke downdraught Weber carburettors and a four-branch exhaust manifold, it produced 78 b.h.p. This was enough to bring its 0–60 m.p.h. time down to less than 11 seconds.

The 4/4 continued to use the 1,500-c.c. Ford engine until the autumn of 1968, when the 1,600-c.c. Ford engine came into use. The word 'series' was dropped from the car's full name and it became the 4/4 1,600. At just about the same time, the Plus-4 range was dropped in favour of the Plus-8, but for details of this car I would refer you to the next chapter. As the Plus-8 was not produced in a four-seater version, a four-seater 4/4 went into production at this time, using the slightly tuned 1,600 G.T. engine. The 4/4 range has comprised three models since 1968: the 4/4 two-seater using a standard 1,600-c.c. engine, a 4/4 two-seater competition model using a 1,600 G.T. engine, and a four-seater competition model.

Although, as I have said, Chris Lawrence's crash in 1966 marked the end of the spectacular post-war period of Morgan competition successes, it would be a great mistake to suppose that there has been nothing doing since then. Morgans are involved in club competitions both at home and abroad almost every weekend of the year, and in this field they are remarkably successful. As recently as 1971 Mr. and Mrs. Morgan won the Motor Cycling Club's triple award. This was as a result of their obtaining premier awards in the club's three most important events of the season: the Land's End, Edinburgh and Exeter trials. Furthermore, in January 1972 a Morgan Plus-8 team consisting of Mr. and Mrs. Morgan, Jim Goodall, Geoff Marketts and Mr. and Mrs. H. Roberts won the team prize in the Exeter trial in very unpleasant weather conditions.

At the time of writing, Chris Lawrence is well advanced in his efforts to tune a Plus-8, and when he has finally perfected the art of getting the most out of the Rover engine, some fine results may be achieved. In any case, the future for Morgans in the competition world looks distinctly exciting.

The Plus·8 from 1966

In 1950, when Morgans brought out the Plus-4, they adopted the excellent 2,088-c.c. Standard Vanguard engine as the power unit. This engine soon became the Triumph TR 2 engine, and with certain technical improvements and slightly altered capacity* it became over the years the TR 3, TR 4 and TR 4A. The crowning glory for this engine came at Le Mans in 1962 when a Lawrencetune Morgan won its class. There can be no doubt that this was a most successful marriage of car and engine, but by late 1965 it was clear that the four-cylinder Triumph engine was becoming obsolescent.

Morgans had always had excellent relations with Standard-Triumph—there was no question of them suddenly being left high and dry without an engine, as Triumph would undoubtedly have continued to produce them in small numbers for Morgans for as long as was necessary. Nevertheless, by early 1966, Peter Morgan was looking out for a new engine. He would probably have liked to continue using Triumph, but the size of the new six-cylinder unit for the Triumph TR 5 made this out of the question: there was no way of fitting it into the Morgan.

Morgans had used Ford engines in some of their cars ever since 1932, and so naturally one of the possibilities examined was the Ford V-6. Morgan was already using the 1,500-c.c. (later 1,600) Cortina engine in the 4/4, but wanted something that would produce a significantly higher power-to-weight ratio in the Plus-4. Unfortunately, when a Ford V-6 was lowered into a Plus-4 it was found to be both too tall and too heavy for the car, and so the search for the ideal power unit continued.

* The Vanguard engine had a capacity of 2,088 c.c., the TR 2 and TR 3 1,991 c.c., and the TR 4 2,138 c.c.

At the end of May 1966, Peter Wilks, a director of Rover, contacted Peter Morgan and came to see him at Malvern. During the visit Wilks put out a gentle feeler to see whether Morgan might consider the possibility of some sort of take-over by Rover. Peter Morgan replied that if his company had to be sold one day he would very much like it to be bought by such a reputable firm as Rover, but nevertheless made it clear that he wanted to soldier on for the present. Another topic that came up at the meeting was the new V-8 engine, as Rover had recently acquired the right to build this from Buick. Peter Morgan had heard something of this engine, but as he knew that Rovers had never supplied power units to outside manufacturers, the idea of using it for the Morgan had never entered his mind. But it struck him immediately that this V-8 engine, being light and compact, could be ideal, and he was very pleased indeed when Wilks said there was a possibility that he could use it.

A racing engineer called Maurice Owen, who had an especially soft spot for Morgans, had twice approached Peter Morgan asking whether he wanted to have any 'specials' built. Each time Peter Morgan had said 'no'. But now, realizing that his staff were too busy to take on the project of building a prototype Morgan with a Rover V-8 engine, and in view of Mr. Owen's great interest in such a scheme, Morgan decided that he would be the ideal man for the job. Maurice was obviously delighted to join Morgans, and the timing was perfect as the Laystall Racing Team for which he had been working had recently been wound up. In the autumn of 1966, Morgan introduced him to some of the engineers at Rover, and work soon began on a prototype in the little research and development hut at Malvern. It immediately became clear that, although it was going to be quite difficult, the Rover engine could definitely be made to fit in the car, as it did not stick up too high and its exhausts came out at a convenient point. In these early weeks Maurice had to be content with a non-working mock-up of a Rover engine, for none was available. This was very frustrating, and when it became clear that there was no chance of an engine before the end of the year, he obtained a Buick engine. He did this quite discreetly so that word would not get out that Morgans were going over to V-8s, and the engineers at Rovers modified the engine to bring it up to their specification. Although Rovers worked from the Buick blueprints, there are certain differences between the two companies' engines and the Rover version is almost certainly the better product. Rover, for instance, stiffened up

The Rover V-8 engine in a Plus-8

the main bearing webs, and sand-cast the blocks instead of die-casting them.

As work on the prototype progressed, it became obvious that a number of modifications were needed. The new engine was wider than the Triumph, so for a start a steering column that would go round the V-8 was required. As this necessitated a new type of steering column, they decided on one of the collapsible models which would fit in with the American Safety Laws, now being discussed for the first time. Maurice therefore adopted the A.C. Delco-Saginaw column, which proved very satisfactory. Next, it became obvious that there was simply no room under the bonnet for an engine-driven fan. Maurice would have preferred this type of fan if it had been possible, since the $1\frac{1}{2}$ b.h.p. which it would have taken from the engine would scarcely have been noticed by the big V-8. Nevertheless, a thermostatically

Maurice Owen and his assistant, Chris, at work in the development department at Malvern

controlled electric fan was fitted.

   In order to carry out the work as simply and as quickly as possible, Maurice used the traditional Morgan principle of 'make first and draw later'. This principle is not entirely peculiar to Morgans for, as Maurice points out, Sydney Camm of Hawker Aircraft built three aeroplanes before doing any serious drawing!

   After a few weeks' work on the project, Maurice, who describes himself as 'a little larger than most', decided that it would be a good idea to use the opportunity of building a new Morgan to increase the body width by two inches. Mr. Morgan readily agreed to this. Later they decided to increase the chassis width as well, and as Rubery-Owen, the chassis builders, would have to retool for this anyway, they decided to lengthen the chassis by two inches at the same time, to make the engine fit a little more easily.

There were difficulties in linking the Buick engine to the Moss unit used by Morgans in the Plus-4. A little research quickly showed that the Moss gearbox was strong enough to stand the very much greater torque provided by the Rover engine, and so Maurice argon-arced the narrow end of a Morgan bellhousing to the broad end of a Buick bellhousing and made a special primary shaft. At the same time he replaced the conventional direct clutch linkage with a small hydraulic slave-cylinder. He then contacted Salisburys— the manufacturers of the Morgan back axle—and asked if they thought their unit would be happy with the new engine. As their response was encouraging, he carried out slight modifications to an axle that was in stock and fitted it.

The new car was obviously going to be that much faster than anything Morgans had produced before, and this made Mr. Owen do some careful thinking about the suspension. He decided that there was no point in moving away from the traditional Morgan sliding-pillar front suspension which was patented in 1910, for even at high speeds this in its modern form continues to give excellent roadholding. But some change was needed in the rear suspension to overcome the possibility of axle-tramp. With this in mind, he dropped the front anchorage of the rear springs by $2\frac{1}{2}$ in. and lifted the rear anchorage to give $7°$ of fall on the spring. At the same time he reduced the chassis under the axle to give a little more rebound on the axle.

As the American Safety Regulations were published in 1967, the timing was almost perfect for Morgans. As soon as the company received details, Maurice Owen and Peter Morgan had a lengthy meeting in which they discussed the best ways to apply them to the car. This was no mean task and Maurice recalls the extreme difficulty of even understanding the regulations, drawn up as they were in complex legal language. Nevertheless, they set to work to find suppliers of the special equipment required, such as rocker switches, and all these features were incorporated in the car.

During his long experience as a racing mechanic, Maurice had come to appreciate the importance of well-designed seating in sports cars, and he had personally been involved in making seats for many drivers, including Stirling Moss and Graham Hill. He therefore used his expertise to build bucket seats of his own design and, having found them satisfactory, took them to Restall who now make them for Morgans. Here again was another successful example of the 'make first, draw later' principle.

By mid-February 1967, the prototype Plus-8 was very

nearly ready, and excitement became so intense in the last few days before it was driven that Maurice found little time for sleep. On 16th February, all that remained was for a Lucas engineer to finish the wiring. He should have completed his job by the end of the afternoon, but a fault developed in the alternator, causing some of the wiring to burn out. As he knew he could not return to Malvern for several days because of other work, the electrician valiantly agreed to finish the job, which meant that he did not leave for home until after 10.30 that night. This left Maurice and his assistant with just a few final adjustments to make, and soon after midnight the Malvern Hills reverberated for the first time to the deep-throated rumble of a Morgan Plus-8.

It was an exciting moment and the car surpassed even the optimistic expectations of Mr. Owen. Peter Morgan never interfered with his work at any time. He had absolute faith in his efforts and this was something Maurice appreciated very much. The next morning Maurice invited Mr. Morgan to try the car and he was very pleased with it. But the completion of the prototype by no means marked the end of difficulties—indeed it was only the beginning.

In January 1967, Rovers were taken over by British Leyland and inevitably this caused a change of policy in many departments. One of the matters affected by the changeover was of course the question of the V-8 engine being supplied to Morgans. Perhaps understandably, the new Rover company did not want to rush any decisions. This was, of course, very unfortunate for Mr. Morgan, as he was at that time hoping to have the Plus-8 ready for launching at the 1967 Motor Show. But, clearly, Rovers did not want to be hurried.

In February, Harry Webster of Standard-Triumph (which had since 1961 also been part of British Leyland) invited Mr. Morgan to lunch, and afterwards took him round the Triumph engine factory and showed him all sorts of engines, including the V-8 unit that was being developed for the Stag. He asked Mr. Morgan if he was interested in any of them, but Morgan replied that his heart was set on the Rover V-8.

A string of delays and difficulties followed, and then Morgan went to see Sir George Farmer, the financial controller of British Leyland, who informed him that it would be necessary to obtain permission from General Motors if Morgans were to use the British engine. Sir George promised to apply for this permission, which was in fact promptly granted, but still the difficulties continued.

In the meantime, Morgan was becoming worried that all the months of development might be wasted if the project fell through, and that more than a year of valuable time might be lost. He therefore invited Harry Webster and George Turnbull down to Malvern in October 1967 and gave them the prototype Plus-8 to try out. They each drove it in turn and were obviously pleased: before leaving, they made it very clear that the arrangement between Morgans and Rovers was definitely on, and that supplies of engines could start being delivered very soon after the launching of the Rover 3,500 in April 1968.

Peter Morgan was delighted, and he and Maurice Owen set to work to carry out an intensive programme of development and improvement in the six months they had left before the car came out. This involved both improving the car before production and also preparing the factory to manufacture the new model.

A number of alterations were made to the car, some of considerable importance. They decided that the increased performance required a more powerful servo-assisted braking system, and this was adopted. The greater fuel consumption suggested that it would be wise to use larger petrol tanks in the Plus-8 than had been used previously, and triple windscreen wipers were also fitted.

The cost of producing the prototype Plus-8 was remarkably small—Mr. Morgan estimates it as being under £3,000—but the expense of preparing the factory to manufacture the car was not inconsiderable. Rubery-Owen charged £1,500 for the retooling required to produce the new type of chassis, and as Mr. Morgan wanted to use specially designed wheels he had to pay £1,200 to have a die cast. The Plus-8 was fitted with electrical equipment unheard of in previous models (except those for American export), such as an alternator, twin spot lamps and hazard warning lights. This meant that a stronger and more complex wiring harness had to be produced. One way and another expenses such as these amounted to over £13,000, and by the time a stock of all parts necessary for the new car had been prepared the total cost had risen to £40,000.

Maurice Owen was confident that the Plus-8 would not suffer from teething troubles and to a great extent he was right, but he and his colleague have made a number of improvements since the car first came out. The increased speed led to increased hood-flap, and this Maurice was able to reduce by making the hood supports rounded instead of flat. He also found that rubber radiator mountings were

Peter Morgan working on blueprints for the Plus-8 at his home in Upton-upon-Severn

more satisfactory than the original inflexible ones, and these are now fitted on all new Plus-8s.

As some owners found the exhaust system rather unsatisfactory, Maurice developed one with a new type of mounting bracket, which has now been incorporated in all

Plus-8s except for those exported to America. He is still hard at work finding ways to make the car even better, and it will be interesting to see what he comes up with in the next few years.

The original prototype Plus-8 (which is Maurice Owen's regular car to this day) does not look exactly like a Plus-8 as we know it. There are bumps in the bonnet to accommodate the carburettors and it has wire wheels. Furthermore, it is 2 in. shorter than proper Plus-8s as it is built on a Plus-4

The first prototype Plus-8

chassis. It is the same width, but this was only achieved by
building the bodywork outwards for an inch on either side
of the chassis. Only one other prototype was ever built and
that was MMC 11, still Peter Morgan's personal car. It was
in all respects like the production Plus-8s except that it had
double and not triple windscreen wipers. MMC 11 was made
available to the press in the late summer of 1968 and the new
model was publicly announced at the end of August.

The motoring press received the new Morgan with enthusiasm. In *Sports Car Graphic*, Phillip Llewellin headed his
article, 'Thoroughly Modern Morgan', having in mind the
film 'Thoroughly Modern Millie' which had been released
a few months previously. But he was writing with his tongue
in his cheek, as his comments about suspension show: 'What
about suspension changes? Best prepare yourself for a shock,

The second prototype Plus-8

The Plus-8 at speed at Silverstone

dear friend, because the Morgan has gone all soft—so soft that it is now just a little difficult to tell whether that cigarette butt which just disturbed the front wheels was plain or filter-tipped. All things, as Einstein told the world, are relative; Morgan's soft is the rest of the industry's granite. The clock ticks slowly at Malvern and it is going to take more than a piddling little 54 per cent power increase to make them abandon the sliding pillars and coils up front, patented by H.F.S. not so very long after Queen Victoria turned up her toes.'

The Autocar also felt the suspension was a little hard: 'You must get used to being jolted hard over every bump in a way that would not have escaped unfavourable comment even before the last war.' But both magazines liked the general feel of the car. *The Autocar* said: 'The driving position is definitely vintage; you sit close to the steering wheel and dash-board but do not feel cramped even if tall.'

On the same topic, *Sports Car Graphic* said: 'The driving position is, as ever, closer to Nuvolari than Graham Hill

The strength of the Plus-8: this one crashed in Sweden at 110 km. The passengers were not seriously hurt

although a leather rimmed steering wheel is a smart and practical gesture towards modernity. There is none of this fancy finger-tip control business. Man!—you really steer the Plus-8 using steely wrists and hairy forearms.'

The aerodynamics of the car also came in for some amusing comments by the same American writer: 'Aerodynamically the Plus-8 is probably little better than Worcester Cathedral, a few miles down the road from Malvern, and this starts extracting its inevitable toll as speeds increase.'

But *Autosport* was of quite another opinion: 'Although the shape does not look very streamlined, the drag must be fairly low, as the car simply flashes up to 120 m.p.h. whether the hood be up or down.'

All critics were generally delighted by the combination of excellent acceleration and braking with traditional vintage feel, and some very sound summaries were written. *The Autocar* had this to say: 'Summing up the Morgan Plus-8 isn't easy. It owes much to that very fine power-unit and

A unique Plus-8: Mrs. Morgan's automatic drophead coupé

becomes a case of new wine in an old bottle. We cannot bring ourselves to disapprove too strongly about the discomforts of the classic style of body (several of us loved this nostalgia as much as anything about this very appealing car) and of course it is one of the reasons for the success of the Morgan, especially in America. . . . Perhaps the spontaneous remark made when slowing hard after an acceleration run at MIRA does the job adequately: "There's a lot which could be better but there's an awful lot right." '

John Bolster was equally friendly in *Autosport*'s summary: 'I always enjoy Morgans because they are cars built for the owner's pleasure. Some makes appeal because of their novel engineering features, but the Morgan endears itself by being predictably the same. With its powerful light-alloy V-8 engine and wide tyres, the latest model is even more typically Morgan than anything that has gone before. This is an exciting sports car with electric acceleration that is glued to the road, at a price which many of us can afford to pay.'

Results in the period since the Plus-8 was launched have shown that the flattering comments in the press were well deserved. But, because Rovers have had to direct so much effort towards controlling exhaust emission in order to be able to sell in America, they have not been able to devote so much energy towards making more highly tuned versions of the engine. Thus, we must expect that it will take as long for the Rover V-8 to develop as it did for the Standard Vanguard engine to be transformed into the Triumph TR 2, TR 3, TR 4 and TR 4A. Morgans used that engine for eighteen years and it did not cease to improve throughout that period. Peter Morgan expects the same to happen with the Rover.

So far the car has only really been able to prove itself on the track in one particular field and that is in Canadian races for completely unaltered production cars. In this field it has done extremely well, and I feel sure we may expect great things in the future.

How Morgans are made

The Morgan Motor Company has a unique and unrivalled place in the motor industry: it produces the only sports car to enjoy the blessing of pre-war body design that has evolved and not been created as a deliberate anachronism. The Fiat Gamine and models produced by the American Replicar company are all unashamedly pre-war-style designs created in the late sixties. The Morgan, by contrast, is the genuine creation of pre-war design carried out in pre-war days, with the added benefit of certain modern technical improvements. If a firm suddenly began to produce cars today of the same design era as that to which the Morgan belongs, no sports car enthusiast could think of them as being anything but a fraud. The reason why Morgan's order book is bursting is that many people believe that British sports car design and production techniques have never surpassed their pre-war standards, and that modern cars are ugly, flashy, ill-made and dull to drive. All those who felt this way did at least until the late fifties have a choice between Morgans and H.R.G.s. The latter firm was founded in the mid-1930s and for the greater part of its life-span produced cars quite similar to four-wheeler Morgans. But since the sad day that H.R.G. closed down, Peter Morgan has been on his own. He is in fact the only man in the motor industry not only to believe in, but also to put into practice, the theory that if his father's techniques made Morgans a much respected name before the war, those same techniques will keep the name respected today.

The Morgan factory has scarcely changed at all since it moved to its present site shortly after the end of the First World War. This makes it a very remarkable place to visit in this age of automation, and in view of this it seems well worthwhile taking a close look at how a Morgan is made.

The factory is situated at the far end of Pickersleigh Road in Malvern Link and in no way detracts from the natural beauty of its setting. When a visitor arrives at the Link Station and begins the five-minute walk up Pickersleigh Road to the factory, he sees a spacious green common on the right stretching away to the foot of the Malvern Hills. The rich greenish-purple colour of these hills at once gives a great sense of romance to the area. Surely nowhere on earth could there be a less likely spot for a car factory?

As the visitor progresses, he comes to a bend in the road and for the first time sees the low, red-brick building bearing the initials 'M.M.'. Here Morgans have been made since the early 1920s when the firm moved out of its original factory, situated almost next to the Link Station, which has since become Bowman and Acock's Garage—the Morgan agents in Malvern.

The factory is entered by the main yard to the right of the building, and it is at once evident that one has come to the right place: this yard always contains a number of half-

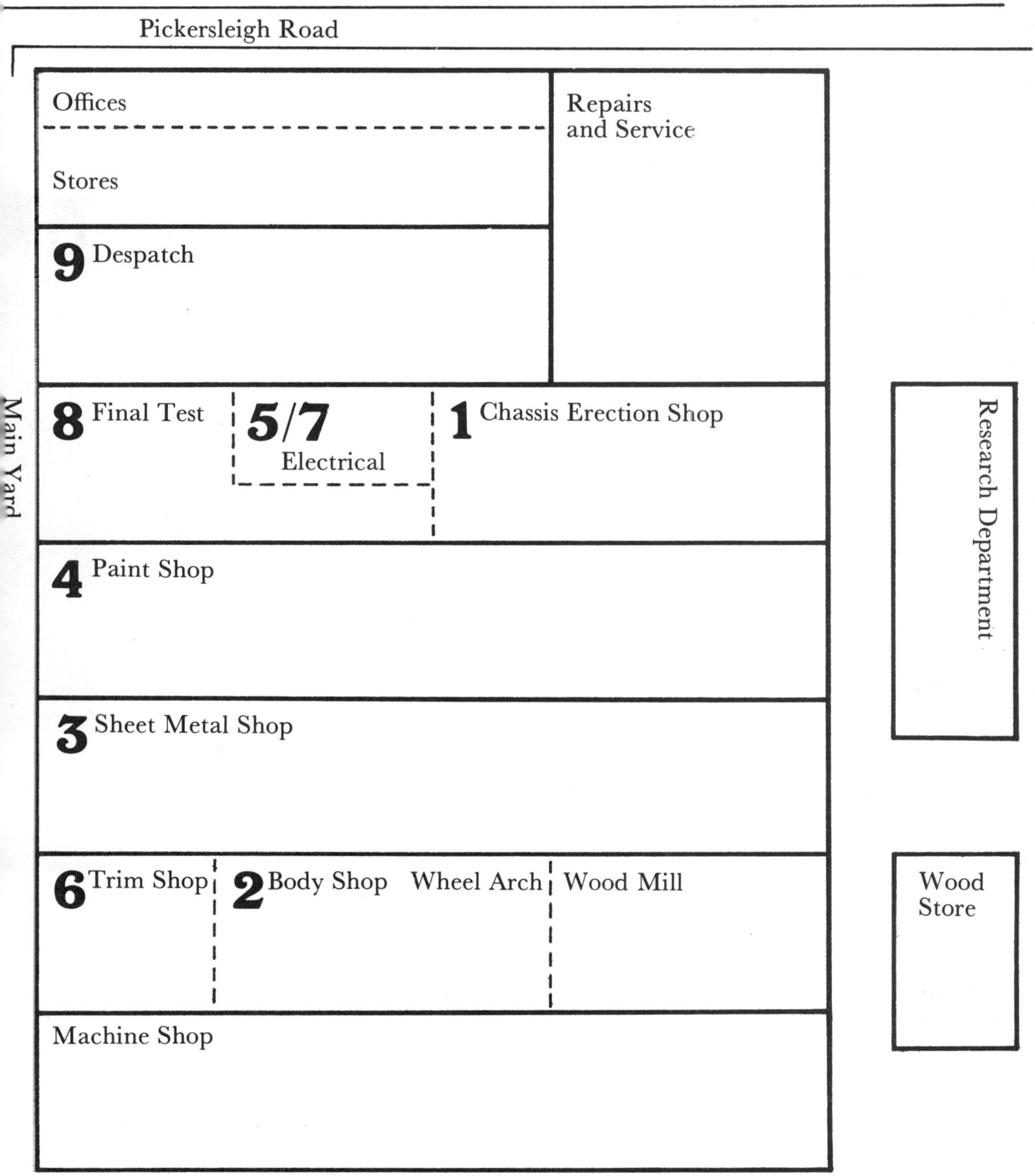

Pickersleigh Road

Main Yard

Offices	Repairs and Service
Stores	
9 Despatch	

8 Final Test   **5/7** Electrical   **1** Chassis Erection Shop

4 Paint Shop

3 Sheet Metal Shop

6 Trim Shop   **2** Body Shop   Wheel Arch   Wood Mill

Machine Shop

Research Department

Wood Store

Factory plan of the Morgan Motor Company as in 1971. The numbers show the order in which cars visit the different parts of the factory

The erecting shop

finished Morgans which I sometimes suspect have been deposited there in transit between two parts of the factory, so that the exhausted porters who move them to and fro can have a rest. Beyond these there is normally parked MMC 11 (Peter Morgan's own Plus-8) and works manager Mr. Goodall's Plus-4 four-seater.

The factory is divided into seven bays, although some of these are further sub-divided inside, and one is immediately amused to reflect that because H.F.S. did not concern himself about the slope of the factory floor, much of the pushing required to move the cars around the factory is uphill work.

The first step in the birth of a new Morgan is taken in the third of the seven bays, when one of the seven factory porters brings a chassis from the stores and lays it on wooden trestles about half-way down the bay on the left. While the chassis is thus being prepared, other workmen in the same bay are putting tyres on wheels and fitting certain parts such as the modified water pump and belt assembly to the engines. In the case of the Rover engine, the bellhousing, primary shaft and gearbox are also fitted at this time. It is normal practice to prepare only the two or three engines at the front of the pile in this way—they are not all prepared in advance as one might expect.

When these preliminaries have been completed, the workmen go to storage racks and select a number of parts, including a foot-pedal set—that is the brake, clutch and accelerator assembly—a handbrake lever and a front suspension frame. They bring these parts back to the waiting chassis and then, using a good do-it-yourself-style electric drill, they bore out the holes needed to fit them. When these first few parts have been fitted, the men get together and carry the chassis over to other trestles on the opposite side of the bay. Here a fitter is quickly on to the job of mounting the front brake pipes, as this can only be done conveniently before the engine is lowered in. When the brake pipes are ready, the engine is lowered on to the chassis by a few strong men using an overhead manually operated pulley. At this stage, a man holding an electric drill—rather larger than the first one—drills the engine mounting holes in the chassis, while others wander hither and thither collecting parts which they lay on or beside the chassis. From something that looks like the bellows of a giant piano-accordion but which in fact is a stack of bulkheads, they take the metal section that covers the driver's and passenger's legs and feet. From other piles come steering columns, shock-absorbers, springs, axles, U-bolts, brake cylinders and wheels already fitted with inflated tyres. When I first began my research for this chapter I was surprised to find that every workman I spoke to described the sequence of operations in a different order. Being a little intrigued by this, I consulted Mr. Goodall, the works manager, who told me that there was no rigid order in which the work in the chassis erection shop was carried out and that it did in fact vary slightly from day to day.

When all that is necessary has been done in the chassis erection shop, the porters are summoned and with a little puffing and blowing they push the car—for it is already beginning to look like a car—out of the door, into the yard and down the gentle slope to the central portion of the sixth bay. This is where the wooden subframe of the body is made and assembled, chiefly from parts made of Belgian ash that have been prepared in the wood-mill at the end of the

The factory porters at work

bay. The ash arrives at the mill kiln-dried so that it can be used at once. The only hazard here is that so much shooting went on in the Belgian forests during the war that a bullet or a piece of shrapnel quite regularly blunts one of the saws. The policy in the mill is to make one kind of part at a time until a stock of forty or so has been built up; thus any one part is only made about once a month. The mill, which has only had one new machine since the war, successfully keeps pace with the rest of the factory and has enough parts left over for spares. The three men who work here know each of the machines so intimately that using forty-year-old equipment does not worry them at all.

Eight men work in the body shop. They begin by gluing a damp course on to the upper surface of the chassis so that the wood is not bolted directly on to the metal. They then finish the parts that have been made in the mill and assemble them

The wood mill at the Morgan factory as it is today, showing some of the wooden parts used in the ash subframe

into complete wooden subframes before bolting them on to the chassis. The wooden door-frames are also made and hung in this shop, each one being individually constructed to fit perfectly. The thick board that protects the underside of the petrol tank is installed with the petrol tank above it and finally the floorboards are fitted. The car is then ready to leave the body shop.

Probably the most intricate work in the body shop is the construction of wheel arches. To make these, thin ash boards are carefully selected and coated with a special hardening acid. Then beetle cement is applied so that they can be laminated and placed in special wooden clamps, ready to go into the drying cupboard three at a time. The clamps are simply made out of carefully shaped pieces of wood held together with stout bolts. After the laminated ash has spent

Finished wooden parts in the wood mill

Glue pots bubbling on the hob in the body shop

Fitting a damp course

Wooden subframes

Clamping up the wheel arches

about nine hours in the drying cupboard it will not lose its shape. In order that supply should meet demand, one batch of wheel arches is placed in the cupboard early in the morning, and when this has been used another batch is put in its place and left overnight.

When the body shop has fulfilled its duties, the factory porters are again called out and they take the car through the trim shop, out into the yard, up the gentle slope and into the fifth bay of the factory—the sheet metal shop. In the little office just inside hangs a photograph of the shop taken in 1927, and it is impressive that a number of the men and machines shown in the picture are still going strong to this day. In this shop the work is done in three main stages. On arrival, the car is handed over to one particular man who makes its rear panels, its quarter panels and its door panels, and then fits them on to the ash subframe. He cuts the panels out of sheets of metal and shapes them individually until they fit the car he is working on perfectly. The panels are numbered so that if at a later stage the work is thought to be sub-standard, it can easily be traced back to the man

The sheet metal shop in 1927. In the bowler hat is Mr. Sambrook, Snr., who was then the foreman

The sheet metal shop in 1971. In the middle is Mr. Sambrook, Jnr., the present foreman

Body panels being hammered into shape

Nailing the body panels on to the ash subframe

responsible. This, however, is an extremely rare occurrence. In those places where panels come into contact with the sub-frame, the edge is turned over at right angles to the panel for about a quarter of an inch, so that tacks may be driven through the sheet metal into the ash without being visible on the side of the car. Thus it is chiefly with tin-tacks and a few screws that the Morgan body is held together, and this system pays good dividends if a crash or corrosion causes a panel to be replaced at some future date.

It takes nearly two days to make the panels for a Morgan. When the job is complete, the car is pushed along the shop to the next man, whose job it is to fit the wings and the front cowl. These are made with the same care and attention as the other parts of the body and are fitted to the car in just the same way. Finally the car is handed over to the bonnet-maker—the man with the trickiest job of all. He begins by taking a sheet of metal measuring 84 in. × 44 in. which is just big enough to make one complete bonnet, with a little to spare. He then cuts the metal into the two halves of the bonnet and puts each half through one of the sets of rollers—which also appear in the 1927 photograph—to shape them. When the bonnet has emerged with the right curvature, it is taken to a machine which bends the top edge of each half in preparation for fitting the hinges. In the final stage, hinges are spot-welded on to the bonnet, and this is the only point in the whole process of manufacturing a Morgan at which a technique so modern as spot-welding is used. The result of all this painstaking effort is a perfect fit for every car; something that no mass-produced car can hope to achieve.

Most Morgan bonnets are made with louvres, although on the current 4/4 models this is an optional extra. To watch the louvres being made is a sight to warm any enthusiast's heart. The machine used for the operation is a fly-press, entirely powered by human muscle. The same machine has been used since soon after the First World War, although the actual cutting part has been replaced more than once in the intervening years. Each louvre is individually made by the machine on pencil marks accurately drawn on the bare sheet metal. It is a slow process and one that causes arm-ache, but this does not worry the louvre makers at Malvern.

At this point I ought to mention one of the other duties that keep the factory porters on their toes. As each car's set of wings is completed, they rush it to the paint shop where all four wings are cleaned off with a special acid. They are then washed and wiped dry prior to being sprayed with a generous coat of primer. The porters collect these wings as

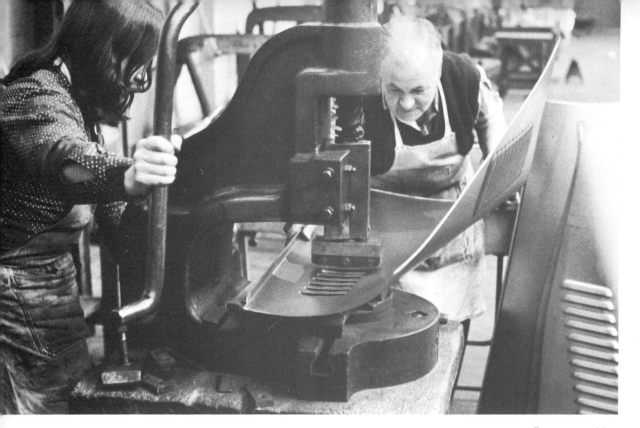

Louvre making

A line-up of Morgan front wings

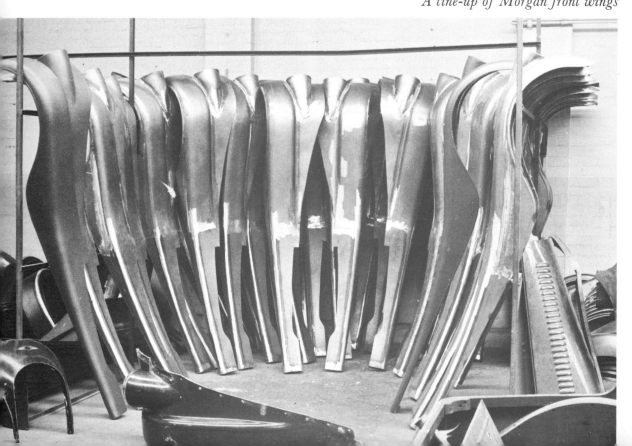

soon as they are dry and hurry them back to the sheet metal shop, to be joined to the car to which they belong. With wings and doors securely mounted, the porters take the car through to the spray shop where all those parts that have not been sprayed with primer are given the acid treatment and cleaned off. The whole car is then sprayed with primer and handed over to one of the Morgan putty experts.

These men have the skill of sculptors and they need it, for they have the extremely tricky task of filling in all the little imperfections in the wings and especially in the welding that holds together the different sections. The shape of the wings makes their task very difficult as any mistake they make will show up badly on the final finish. Once the putty has been applied, it is smoothed down. The men who do the job are convinced that any kind of sanding machine would have a disastrous effect at this stage, so they do all the rubbing down by hand, using different grades of silicone paper. When these sculptors have finished, the whole car is given two or sometimes three coats of a grey paint called primer surfacer; the wings are always given an extra one or two coats of this, being the most exposed parts of the car. As soon as these coats have been applied, black paint is sprayed all over the

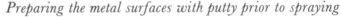

Preparing the metal surfaces with putty prior to spraying

Sewing in the trim shop

inside of the car and underneath the wings. Underseal is also normally applied at this time.

When the coats of primer surfacer have dried overnight, they are carefully rubbed down with a fine-grain silicone paper—all by hand of course—and then undercoat is applied. When this too has had a chance to dry, it is given the silicone paper treatment and then the finishing coat is applied. There are always at least two coats of this, but as some colours cover better than others, up to six coats are sometimes applied so that the sprayers can feel fully satisfied.

I am sure that the reader will have no difficulty in guessing what happens next—the porters are called in again and this time their assignment is to take the gleaming machine through to the electrical shop for a fleeting visit. I say fleeting visit because only a small part of the electrical work can be done at this stage. The lights are fitted and wired up and the harness is installed and loosly clipped into position; but that is all. With many parts of the car displaying what looks like bundles of coloured spaghetti, those busy porters are called back again to move the half-wired car to the trim shop so that the upholstery can be put in place before the electricians complete their task.

In the trim shop, the wires are covered with the upholstery
and the wheel arches, rockers and door panels are fitted. The
intricate leatherwork which covers the gearbox and transmission tunnel is cut to shape, stitched and fitted, and in the
case of 4/4 models, the seats are made here too—although in
the Plus-8 externally manufactured seats are used. The trim
shop has a staff of nine, including three jolly ladies who
work away on the slightly antiquated sewing machines. All
the upholstery, including tonneau and hood, is individually
made for the car to which it is fitted. Nothing is pre-cut or
ready-made, so that everything again fits perfectly.

Perhaps the smallest department—if one can call it a
department—in the Morgan factory is where the windscreens are fitted. This, happily, is so near the trim shop that
those hard-worked porters are not required here. With the
windscreen in place, the car is collected by the squad of
porters and taken via the yard to the electrical bay where
the wiring-up is completed and all the spaghetti is neatly
tucked away out of sight. In the old days, the electricians
had an extremely difficult task, as every electrical part on
the three-wheelers had its own separate wire. Today,
thanks to the colour-coded harness which Morgans have
made up for them, their job is much simpler although not
entirely hazard-free. It does occasionally happen that, when
the electrical system of a new Morgan is first tested with a
battery, a fine shower of sparks flies out. On these occasions
the cause is usually a tin-tack driven through the harness
by an over-enthusiastic trimmer.

After its second visit to the electrical shop, the newly born
car is very nearly complete and in some cases cars are handed
over at this stage to the chief tester. More often, however,
they are wheeled back to the finishing shop, which is in the
same bay as the trim shop. Here the final touches are
applied: these include fitting the bumpers, the sidescreens,
and the Morgan badges. The car is then transferred to the
test shop, where it is handed over to one of the most envied
men in the Morgan world—the chief tester. At present
this job is held by Charlie Curtis, now well into his seventies
and wonderfully well qualified for the job. He began as a
mechanic in the test department of Morgans shortly after the
end of the First World War, and swiftly rose to the post of
chief tester. Thus Charlie Curtis has, with very few excep-
tions, driven every Morgan that has been made since 1927.
Normally Charlie drives without hood or sidescreens—
because he likes it that way—and his regular run is about
ten miles, carefully selected to include some twisty sections

Charlie Curtis—the chief tester 1947–71

of Worcestershire country roads, some hills and some comfortable straight stretches. Surprisingly enough, Charlie never remembers having had to telephone the Works for help during his test runs—he has always managed to get back even when things have gone wrong. However, he does remember breaking starting handles on a few occasions.

When Charlie Curtis returns from his run, his mechanic colleagues carry out any adjustments which have shown themselves to be necessary, and then off he goes again. I do not think I have ever envied a man his job as much as I envy Charlie Curtis. I am sure that there are raw January days when other means of employment may seem preferable; but to spend the spring and summer driving spanking new Morgans round the beautiful lanes of Worcestershire seems almost too good to be true. If the second test run proves satisfactory, the car is considered ready for despatch. It is therefore driven to the despatch bay where it awaits collection either by its owner or by transporter.

The despatch bay is a most wonderful sight, only equalled by the car-park of the Abbey Hotel in Malvern before one of the Morgan Sports Car Club's annual dinners. It is a long, rather narrow garage, with a row of Morgans of every con-

The despatch bay

ceivable colour parked at 45° to the walls on either side. It is such a thoroughly appetizing sight that the visitor has considerable difficulty in tearing himself away.

In common with most other car firms with an extremely small annual production, Morgans have to buy many parts from other manufacturers. It would, for example, be absurd for them to try to produce their own engines or gearboxes. Nevertheless, the Malvern factory has a most impressive if antiquated machine shop run by Taffy Burston. Mr. Burston is not a Welshman; he was born in Malvern but was brought up by his aunt in Wales and so is known as Taffy. He joined Morgans before H.F.S. was married and had been with the firm for some years by the time it moved to its present factory in 1920.

Almost all the machinery in Taffy's shop dates from 1940, although a few machines are earlier. During the war, the shop produced aircraft parts, achieving an extremely high standard of accuracy, and while many of the one hundred machines installed there by the Government in 1940 were removed at the end of the war, H.F.S. purchased the thirty or so which remain. The equipment—most of it stamped 'War finish — quality as usual'—comprises capstan lathes,

Taffy Burston (left), Morgan's longest serving employee. He joined the firm in 1916 and is now foreman of the machine shop

milling machines, drills and grinders, and these are used to produce the hubs for wire wheels, suspension damper blades, automatic lubrication rams, transmission shafts and pedal sets. They also do all the machining for the clutch bell-housing, brake drums and clutch plunger cases. Almost all the small parts of the car are specially made here, such as the front suspension lugs and handbrake levers, and Morgans even find it worth their while to machine many of their own nuts and bolts.

Years of constant use are beginning to have their effect on some of the lathes and one operator told me that her machine had a tendency to taper. She was so used to this that she found no difficulty in compensating for it. Indeed, it seems that she found this the most interesting aspect of her job. None of the machines is in any way automated or programmed and it seems that this is how the Morgan workers like it.

At the far end of the machine shop is what appears to be and what to all intents and purposes is a blacksmith's hearth. This is where all the mild steel brackets and U-bolts are shaped. Finally, in the brazing department, spare wheel carriers, bumper brackets and seat frameworks are assembled.

The machine shop has a staff of one dozen men and women and, like the wood-mill, manufactures each individual part only rarely. Indeed a year's supply of some parts, such as rear spring hanger bolts, can be made at one time. On the other hand, the complex machining of hubs goes on almost without interruption through the year.

Another important department in the Morgan factory is the repair bay where anything from a regular service to a complete rebuild can be undertaken. The advantage of sending one's Morgan here is that specialists are available to attend to every part of the car, whereas many garages are shy of undertaking such jobs as mending the woodwork or upholstery. Parts can, where necessary, be made up on the spot and all the work is carried out under the watchful eye of Mr. Jay the service manager and well-known former competition driver. He has been with Morgans since 1927. The repair bay is often the resting-place of Peter Morgan's Ferrari and the Morgan mechanics have, over the years, grown quite used to coping with this exotic Italian V-12. Another car of great interest often to be seen in the repair bay (and I am not suggesting that this is because it is often going wrong) is the first prototype Plus-8 belonging to Maurice Owen.

The repair bay used to be home of the research and development department of Morgans. However, when work was beginning on the Plus-8, Mr. Morgan became worried about security, so now Maurice Owen and his extremely discreet colleagues have been banished to a little hut in the back yard.

Thus a close look at the Morgan factory shows that like the Morgan car it has a pre-war flavour, high standards, great individuality and generates plenty of enthusiasm.

The Business History

It is really quite astonishing that in this age of giant companies and automation a very small family-owned car company can still be going strong after more than sixty years of trading. There have, of course, been difficult times, yet Morgan has seen almost all its direct competitors go to the wall and has survived as the world's oldest privately owned car company. The remarkable fact of its survival is not primarily caused by good luck, although that has played its part; it is more because the company has followed sound policies from the very start and has never been tempted to gamble on the future. As the survival of the company is so remarkable it seems a good idea to take a close look at the way the business has been conducted over the years. Sadly, the records are not as complete as might be hoped and it is, therefore, impossible to give as many figures from the early years as one would wish. Nevertheless, the wisdom of the Morgan family and the soundness of their business sense is very evident in any examination of the company, and the firm has to this day an outstanding reputation for correctness and courtesy with all its associates in the motor industry.

As we have seen in the chapter on the early history, the original financial backing for the company came from George Morgan who, although a vicar, had sufficient private means to be able to put up £3,000. This sum was enough to buy a site in Worcester Road, Malvern Link, and to build the original Morgan factory. It bought the machine tools—the drilling machines, lathes and grinders necessary to build the car—and the gas engines needed to drive them (for scarcely any machines were self-powered in those days). Finally, there was just enough money left to provide the working capital for the firm, although this was supplemented by the advance deposits which H.F.S. obtained on each car ordered.

The original Morgan factory, as it is now. Peter Morgan was born in the house on the right

At the time of the foundation of the firm, the Morgan three-wheeler was of a very simple motorcycle-type construction. This meant that all connections between the steel tubes of which it was constructed had to be made with lugs of malleable steel or brass. Each of these had to be machined before they could be brazed on to the chassis. Furthermore, at the beginning of the century there were far fewer specialist suppliers to the motor industry than there are now, so that a new car firm such as Morgan had to be equipped to make almost all parts of the car for itself. Thus, a well-equipped machine shop was absolutely indispensable.

The Morgan first appeared at the Motor Cycle Show in 1910, but only four orders were taken on that occasion. Nevertheless, these, together with the orders that began to come in from Harrods and from friends of the Morgan family, were just enough to get production going until competition successes and improvements in the design could bring in orders in larger quantities.

The business was given a considerable boost in 1911 when H.F.S. entered his car in the Motor Cycle Club's London to Exeter trial and won a gold medal and, at last, in 1912 the company made its first profit—£1,314. Even those who did not have access to the company's books could see that the business was going well by 1912: a number of small huts began to appear behind the main factory building, to alleviate the acute shortage of floor-space caused by the high rate of production. However, the cost of these buildings cannot have been at all great since they did not house any equipment. The car was, of course, hand-painted right up until the Second World War so that such departments as the paint shop only required a few pots of paint and some brushes.

1913 was the first year in which real money was made by the company. According to *The Daily Post* of June 1915, Morgans made a profit of £4,797 in that year, and in 1914, in spite of the coming of war, they more than doubled this figure to £10,450. During the war much of the factory's efforts were concentrated on the production of shells and munitions. Although this work was probably a little less profitable than car production had been, there can be no doubt that the company flourished during the war years, receiving such fringe benefits as government help towards the cost of new equipment for the machine shop. In fact, H.F.S. was to a great extent a pacifist and there was a part of him which was deeply upset by the thought of making money out of the war. But the government's fixed profit allowance for munitions contractors was generous, and he knew he would be a fool to try to do without it.

The repair bay remained in full use throughout the war and car production continued on a small scale. New car development was also able to continue and the first few months of the war saw the construction of a prototype four-wheeler which, however, came to nothing. Later in the war, a prototype Aero model and Family model were built and produced in small quantities. When severe restrictions were imposed on supplying cars for the home market and petrol became impossible to obtain except for work of national importance, Morgans began to export the few cars they were able to produce to the most remarkable places: records show that these included Russia, India and Peru.

The First World War had begun just as Morgan sales were at an all-time high and so, with the advent of peace in 1918, H.F.S. determined to get back into full production as quickly as possible. He succeeded in this objective and the Malvern factory was possibly the very first car factory in the country to return to normal. This had a very important effect on the whole future of Morgans, as it was a time when people wanted cars desperately and could not get them.

Almost any price was acceptable to frustrated would-be motorists, and the Morgan cost more pro-rata for the three years following the end of the war than at any other time in its history.

Before the war Morgan prices had begun at 85 guineas, yet by 1920 the cheapest was the Sporting model at £170 and the most expensive was the Aero at £190. By July 1921 the cheapest was the Grand Prix Standard model at £218 and the most expensive the Aero at £250 or £275 with dynamo lighting. Compare this with a price list of 1933, where the cheapest car was the two-speed Family model at £80 and the most expensive cost £125, and it can be seen how profitable were the early post-war years.

There were several reasons why Morgan was able to get back into production so quickly. The factory was such a compact unit that it was very easy to reorganize quickly. Another factor was the simplicity of the car and the location of the engine outside at the front, which enabled them to use almost any V-twin unit that was available. All V-twins had the same sort of banjo-shaped crank-case, and consequently some special plates were all that was needed to bolt any particular make of engine on to the front chassis tubes. Engines were by no means easy to obtain during this period and it was, therefore, important that Morgans should not be entirely dependent on any one supplier if they were to exploit the scarcity value of transport at this time. Indeed, this was one of the periods in which H.F.S. built up the reserves which carried him through the leaner years that were to come.

Post-war prosperity enabled H.F.S. to complete a new factory very soon after the Armistice was signed, and before the end of 1919 it was being used for all the finishing work. The production of the chassis and all the machining was carried out in Worcester Road. Then, when the cars were on their wheels, they were loaded on to an old Crossley lorry and transported to the Pickersleigh Road factory, where the body was assembled and painted and the upholstery work carried out. This arrangement continued until the Pickersleigh Road factory was considerably extended in 1922, and early in 1923 the whole works was united under one roof with the exception of the machine shop which did not move until 1929.

The fact that all the capital for buying the site and building the new factory came out of H.F.S.'s own pocket, and was not borrowed, is a fair indication of the company's success in these years. Visible signs of prosperity began to appear in

Pourquoi acheter une grosse moto et un sidecar ?
Pour le même prix vous pouvez avoir un

40.000
véhicules
en circulation
la meilleure

garantie

La grande marque de vrai Cyclecar

Type Sporting (tous frais compris). **6.500** fr.
Type Sport (vitesse 100 à l'heure). **6.850** fr.

R. DARMONT, Constructeur à **COURBEVOIE**
27, Rue Jules-Ferry - Tél. 525

Magasin de Vente : 26, Avenue de la Grande-Armée
PARIS - 17ᵉ

An advertisement for the French Morgan, 1923

H.F.S.'s private life too. In 1921 he bought himself a Rolls-
Royce, and in 1925 he moved to a considerably larger house
in Malvern Link called Fern Lodge, which has since become
Seaford Court School.

1921 brought the first post-war recession, but although
many car manufacturers went on to short time, Morgan
continued production at the full rate—something in the
region of 2,500 cars per year. In addition to these, several
hundred Morgans were produced under licence every year
in France by the French concessionaires Darmont and
Badelogue. The agreement had been made in 1919 and provided H.F.S. with a useful source of income. W. G.
McMinnies' success at the Amiens Grand Prix of 1913 was
still remembered in France, so the Darmont Morgan sold
well from the start, and soon began to acquire competition
successes of its own in the hands of M. Darmont. It was
estimated that a total of 40,000 English and French Morgans
had been produced by 1924.

By 1923 the post-war boom was over and competition
was extremely fierce, especially since the advent of the mass-
produced Austin Seven. H.F.S. therefore displayed some of
that remarkable wisdom for which he has always been
renowned: although his order book was completely full, he
began to cut back his production and lower his prices so that
he would not suddenly be caught out unprepared with
quantities of unsold cars on his hands. The Morgan price
range, which in 1921 had been £218–£250, was by 1925
down to £95–£160. He also began to think carefully about
how best to alter the car in order to be sure of preserving his
own special niche in the market. He decided that the way
to do this was to keep the car very sporting but make it a
little more sophisticated. Thus from 1922, front wheel
brakes became available as an optional extra and more and
more cars were fitted with electric light and self-starters. All
this ensured that the Morgan kept pace with cars like the
Austin Seven, while retaining the great advantage of far
better performance. H.F.S. constantly reminded the public
of his cars' sporting abilities, both by entering personally in a
great many trials and competitions and by ensuring that
help was readily available from the factory for all those who
wanted to race Morgans.

It is possible that the advent of the Austin Seven did in
fact help Morgans in one respect: it made H.F.S. reduce the
scale of his business in good time before the Great Depression
began in the late 1920s, and enabled the firm to prosper at a
time when many other car companies were obliged to close

down. Bentley had to sell out to Rolls-Royce in 1931 and by 1935 Swift, Invicta and Star had all come to an end, while Sunbeam and Talbot were snapped up by the Rootes Group.

Morgan's survival in the 1930s seems even more remarkable when one considers that, quite apart from the difficulties caused by the depression, they had to face a lot of new and direct competition. In 1929 B.S.A. introduced their own three-wheeler and produced it at a rate of about 2,000 per year, until 1936 when this division closed down with considerable losses. The failure was caused by the fact that B.S.A. made their three-wheeler almost too refined for their customers* and their attempts to maintain their position vis-à-vis Morgan in the competition world were not crowned with success. In 1933, B.S.A. went over to a four-cylinder engine as did Morgans, but while the Morgan F-type quickly became popular and remained so, the B.S.A. was very severely hit by the taxation changes of 1935, which reduced the cost of road-fund licences on all classes of vehicle except three-wheelers.

Another new direct competitor in the early 1930s was the Raleigh three-wheeler. This originally appeared in 1931 as a tri-van in which the driver sat on a saddle and steered with handlebars. In 1934 it appeared in a far more sophisticated form as the Raleigh Safety Seven. By the time about three thousand of these had been made, Sir Harold Bowden found that, as with the B.S.A., the taxation changes of 1935 had made his cars cease to be a profitable business. He therefore sold his car division to T. L. Williams who began to make commercial three-wheelers in Tamworth under the name of Reliant.

Although neither the depression nor the taxation changes of 1935 could put Morgans out of business, these years were nevertheless very difficult. While the company did not actually lose money, it did no more than break even at this time.

Peter Morgan recalls that someone said to H.F.S. at the Motor Cycle Show one day: 'You're a lucky man, Harry, you can make cars as a hobby.' H.F.S. did not look pleased at this, and later he said to Peter: 'Even if this had been true for me, which it wasn't, you can take it that it will never be true for you.' I mention this because it sums up H.F.S.'s attitude. He was business-minded and clearly would not have kept the company going, much as he loved it, if the bad years had begun to outweigh the good ones. He would

* See Michael Sedgwick, *Cars of the 1930s* (Batsford).

never have let the company eat into his personal reserves, although he accepted that it could not be indefinitely profitable and so built up reserves.

By 1935 the F-model had become what was virtually the ultimate in three-wheelers. Very little was left that could be done to make it more sophisticated: it had a four-cylinder engine, a three-speed gearbox with reverse, self-starter, electric lights and so on. Furthermore, the tide of depression was just beginning to turn in 1935 and it seemed likely that some of those people who had had to put up with a three-wheeler during the hard times would now want to move on to something more expensive. With these thoughts in mind, H.F.S. began to feel that the next logical step was to produce a four-wheeler. He had, after all, produced a prototype, in 1915, although nothing more had been done about it, and the F-type Morgan had of course a normal car-type chassis. In fact, H.F.S. acted only just in time, for while 659 three-wheelers were sold in 1934, only 286 were sold in 1935 and, after all, production of four-wheelers only began right at the end of the year. It is hard to see how the company would have survived 1936 if it had not by then had an excellent four-wheeler to offer—its three-wheeler sales in that year came to only 137 cars. In a sense it was unfortunate that Morgans had to launch the 4/4 at this time, for it meant that the company barely had three full years of production before the Second World War. Yet considering that only 29 three-wheelers were sold in 1939, it is clear that the 4/4 saved Morgans from disaster at this time.

Soon after the outbreak of war, Morgan's machine shop was once again in great demand for war work, all of which was highly profitable, and car production ceased. Those bays which were not used by the company during the war were let for quite satisfactory rents to Flight Refuelling and the Standard Motor Company. The latter began to make carburettors there, and Morgans themselves continued to run the machine shop, the repair bay and the offices and stores.

The company entered the war in a healthy state financially—the late thirties had been quite fruitful years and the 4/4, which had cost so little to develop, had already shown itself to be quite profitable. Once again H.F.S. found himself with a bad conscience over making money out of the war but, nevertheless, realized that there was no alternative. When the war ended, he found that the revenue from the machine shop and the bays that were let had left the company's reserves in good order.

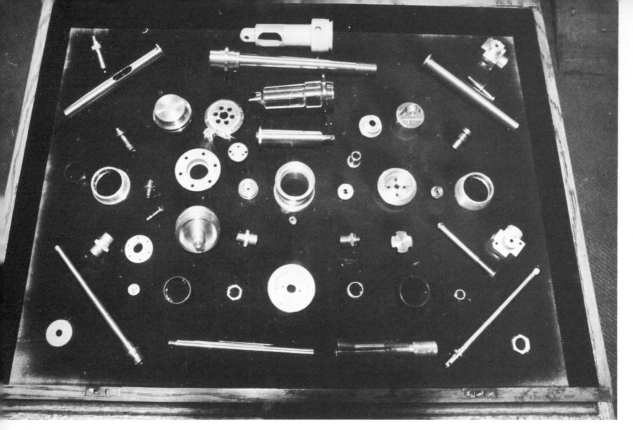

Aircraft parts machined by Morgans during the Second World War

Unfortunately Morgans were not able to begin production anything like as quickly after the Second World War as after the First, and there were a number of reasons for this. The firm was at a great disadvantage in having some of its bays let out to other people, neither Flight Refuelling nor Standard Motors being in a position to move out the very moment the war ended. Even when they did move out early in 1946, very considerable reorganization was required before the shops could return to normal. Another problem was that the labour force drifted back very much more slowly than had been the case in 1918, and it was almost eighteen months before the whole flock was reunited at Malvern. It is in any case arguable that even if there had been a full labour force available in early 1946, production would have been impossible because outside suppliers were in no position to meet the company's requirements.

However, 1946 was not a wasted year. The war had resulted in many machine shops throughout the country being put out of action by bomb damage, so that those which remained could find all the work they wanted and more besides. Thus the machine shop continued to make money for the company, while the rest of the staff was employed in reorganizing the factory and preparing it for full production to begin again at the end of the year. In addition to this a small number of cars were made up out of spare parts from stock and sold.

The machine shop, which held its certificate of competence to manufacture aircraft parts right up until 1960, benefited considerably from the war. The government installed nearly 100 machines there during the war and H.F.S. was later able to buy a number of these at a very reasonable price. Morgans have always had an excellent maintenance staff and so, although these machines had been worked hard throughout the war, they were still in first-class condition. Being able to re-equip the factory at such little cost was one of the few valuable perks brought along by the war.

The post-war era, however, faced Morgans with one requirement which had not existed before, and that was the need to export. As Michael Sedgwick says, British industry was geared to the home market before the war and export was unnecessary. On average during the 1930s, for example, only 20 per cent of the cars produced in England were sent abroad, yet in 1949, 257,922 of the 412,290 cars made, or 62.5 per cent, were exported. Even as late as 1954, more than half the total national production of cars was still going overseas. The war left England seriously short of steel and Morgans found that they could only secure an allocation if they exported the cars which they made out of it. The company therefore began to set up agencies abroad. The first were established in America and France in 1948, but the foreign markets showed no interest whatsoever in three-wheelers; partly perhaps, because three-wheelers do not enjoy the tax benefits abroad that they receive here. It was largely as a result of this experience that H.F.S. dropped three-wheeler production altogether early in 1952.

The 1950s were good years for Morgans, although the business was in one sense rather precarious: it was almost entirely dependent on the American market. Nevertheless, when Sir John Black of Standard-Triumph made a generous offer for Morgans in 1954, H.F.S. was optimistic enough about the future to say 'No'. At this time, the company was producing the Morgan Plus-4 and it seems that Sir John may well have thought of using it as an additional Triumph sports car.

In 1955 Morgans brought back the 4/4. They did this for two reasons: firstly, because they were unable to obtain enough Standard Vanguard engines for the Plus-4, and secondly, because the company had always aimed to produce

Peter Morgan in his office

a really cheap sports car. The 4/4 was, in fact, easily the
cheapest sports car on the market until Austin-Healey
brought out the frog-eyed Sprite in 1958, and the Plus-4
gave the best performance in its price-range. Yet, in spite of
all this, the home and European markets were very poor in
these years.

By the mid-1950s, Morgans were beginning to look old-
fashioned. People had not at that time acquired the affection
for 1930's-style designs that they have now, and while the
motoring press attacked Morgan more and more violently
for their lack of change, the public showed its disapproval
by taking no interest in the Morgan stand at the Motor
Show. Indeed Peter Morgan remembers two or three years
in which he was left all alone on his stand for hours at a time.
In spite of all this, he continued to believe that his design
was good and his judgement was proved sound when,
towards the end of the decade, more and more people began
to flock to his stand again.

But a stand thronged with young people at Earls Court
did not mean that the car sold well at home, and this was

why, as late as 1960, 85 per cent of the factory's production
was going to the United States. As a result of this the collapse
of the American market in 1961 brought along one of the
most serious crises that Morgan has ever had to face.

1961 was the year of the presidential election in which
John F. Kennedy was elected and, for some strange reason,
Americans are never in the mood to buy cars during an
election campaign. In 1961 they were even less in the mood
than usual. But it was not the election that was the prime
cause of the trouble. The real cause of the collapse of the
sports-car market was the great recession in the Californian
aircraft industry, which hit hard at the States' prosperity.
M.G. and Triumph were so hard hit that their agents were
reduced to holding auction sales in order to get rid of the
cars they were stuck with. The Morgan agent resisted the
temptation to do this but, nevertheless, it took him more
than a year to sell the dozen or so cars he had in stock. This
agent had in good years taken as many as 120 of the 350
Morgans produced annually at that time, so the fact that
he suddenly placed no orders for fifteen months could
scarcely fail to cause grave concern at Malvern.

Quite by chance, Peter Morgan and his wife were visiting
America when the first effects of the crisis were beginning
to be felt. The timing of their trip was certainly both
fortunate and a freak, as they had never visited the States
before (neither had H.F.S.). The factory cabled Peter
Morgan in California and informed him that they had had
word from New York cancelling the latest shipment. Morgan
at once cabled back ordering the shipment to be sent off,
explaining that he was going to New York to try to help
matters. In New York he was able to persuade the agent to
accept the shipment and his visit gave him the opportunity
of meeting many American enthusiasts. This in turn led to a
revival of interest and the Eastern American market
gradually improved.

Back in England, Morgan reduced production by one
car a week for a period which lasted for nearly two years,
representing a fall in production of 14 per cent. This was a
typical Morgan gesture, strongly reminiscent of H.F.S.'s
order to cut back production in the 1920s when the Austin
Seven threatened the firm's prosperity. Morgan used the
two years to try to recentre his business and extend his
markets, so that he would never again be so heavily dependent on sales in any one country. He set up enthusiastic
agencies in Canada, Australia and Europe, and was greatly
helped by the fact that people throughout Europe were at

The Board: Maurice Owen, Jim Goodall, Cecil Jay, Peter and Jane Morgan

last beginning to realize that the Morgan was one of the very few cars still in existence which had real character. Agencies established in Switzerland, Sweden, Spain, Austria, Germany and Belgium in the early 1960s were all taking cars in quite reasonable numbers by 1965. Then, finally, the home market began to wake up too. It is most curious that we were the last country in the world to show real enthusiasm after the war for this most English of cars!

One contributory factor to the revival of the home market in the early 1960s, was the appearance in 1964 of the Plus-4-Plus. As Mr. Morgan said: 'So many press people for so many years said "Morgans will never change", that when we did bring out the Plus-4-Plus they thought "My God, they *can* change!"'

Unfortunately the Plus-4-Plus was a flop in as much as it only ran to 50 cars, but in arousing fresh interest in the market it was a great success. When comparing the traditional Morgan with the Plus-4-Plus, people were bound to become enthusiastic about the traditional car, so that the project ended up having the effect of an enormous advertising gimmick (which of course it was not!). As the company did not lose any money on the 50 cars they produced, Peter Morgan had good reason to be well satisfied with the whole scheme. The other factor which also contributed greatly to the revival of interest was the outstanding success of the Lawrencetune Morgan, which won its class at Le Mans in 1962. As with the Plus-4-Plus this provided much good publicity which was very valuable.

Not long after the launching of the Plus-4-Plus, the Morgan family set to work to sort out its financial position. H.F.S., being a great family man, had left the business in trust to his four daughters and his son, with Peter Morgan and Major Kendall as trustees. Peter Morgan was left in charge of the firm. By 1964, it was felt advisable within the family to arrange a capital redistribution of the shares, and this involved making the firm cease to be a limited liability company for a few years. This in fact lasted until 1970, when the writing paper once again sported the word 'Limited' and a board of directors was appointed, consisting of Mr. and Mrs. Morgan, Mr. Jay, Mr. Goodall and Mr. Owen.

The launching of the Plus-8 was a costly process, but the company was fortunate enough not to need to seek outside financial help. To have done so would have been strictly contrary to H.F.S.'s policy. Happily, time has shown that the company's investment in the Plus-8 project was a very wise one.

The prospects for the future are certainly good, although such problems as the uncertainty of the American market are already looming up on the horizon. It is impossible to be sure that the 1975 Federal laws may not cause the cessation of all Morgan imports into the U.S.A., but even this should not be too grave for them. Their sound business policies, like their front suspension, have proved their worth for more than sixty years now and there is every likelihood that they will continue to do so for a long time to come.

Morgans in the Modern World

Most people accept that Morgan holds a unique position in the motoring world, but just what is that position and who is really going for Morgans today? These questions are important to Morgan enthusiasts so I will make some attempt to answer them.

Since the mid-1960s, more Morgans have been sold in England than in any other country, so let us begin by looking at the home market. The majority of Morgans in England are ordered by enthusiasts who want a real sports car with six decades of competition behind it, because they want a car that is interesting and exciting to drive and because they value the fact that it is hand-built to the highest standards. Some of these people feel they want a car they can enter for competitions, and they do not need to spend a long time investigating to discover that Morgans are one of the most successful makes in club competitions. But it is by no means only the enthusiast who fancies himself as a budding Stirling Moss who goes for Morgans. Our local doctor recently acquired a four-seater for doing his rounds and is delighted with it. Nor is he an exception, for there is another doctor in Kent who speeds from one patient to another in a yellow Plus-8. In fact there are a surprising number of Morgans in the hands of businessmen, lawyers and other professional people, and the reason for this seems to be that they are great individualists.

England has its share of film-star owners too—among the most famous being Mick Jagger and Sheila Hancock—but

A G.P. in Buckinghamshire, with the car he uses to do his rounds

One sort of Morgan owner—the King's Road Set

although Morgans used at one time to advertise themselves as the 'Film Star Car' this does not seem to be the true image in this country.

There can be little doubt that Morgan enjoys a more enthusiastic following among the young in England than almost any other car except, perhaps, Lotus, although its price sometimes makes it impossible for young people to own one. Nevertheless, the products of Malvern Link are much in evidence in the King's Road and Carnaby Street, and one Motor Show review came close to the truth when it described the Plus-8 as a 'rustic from the Malvern Hills that has become the darling of the King's Road'.

As there are more Morgans on the roads of England than in any other country, it is only natural that the ownership should be more varied here than anywhere else. As far as Peter Morgan is concerned, he is happy for anyone who loves a Morgan to own one, although he is far more pleased when people tell him that they have bought one because it is a fine piece of engineering than because it is 'way-out' or quaint.

Abroad, reaction to the Morgan seems to vary considerably from country to country, but in most parts it produces as much enthusiasm as in England. According to Morgan's Paris agent, there seems to be a definite cycle in sales of the car in France: it begins when real car enthusiasts buy it because they love vintage cars with a pedigree of generations of successful competition cars behind them. As a result of this, the marque becomes known and all sorts of fashionable and trendy people begin to buy it. Then, when the sports-car lovers see that the Morgan has become so chic, they stop buying it, and for a while the jet-set acquires all the Morgans in France. Finally, the fashion shifts and the Morgan ceases to be the great thing for the jet-set types, so the sports-car lovers begin buying again and the cycle is repeated.

The Savoyes have sold Morgans in France since 1953, and for a few years, they did well. Then, in 1959, sales fell right off until enthusiasts again became keen on the car in about 1962. From 1965 to 1966 all sorts of famous personalities began to buy Morgans, until all three leading French film actresses owned one: Brigitte Bardot, Catherine Deneuve and Anna Carena. On the male side of the acting profession, the leading supporter was Jean-Paul Belmondo.

It was an exciting moment, no doubt, when M. Savoye answered the telephone in his Paris office and found that Miss Bardot's private secretary was on the other end of the line, inquiring about Morgans. Also, no doubt, Miss Bardot was a little surprised that the Morgan factory would not allow her a discount—something that most car firms are delighted to do when someone as famous as Bardot is interested in their products—but she was not discouraged. Not even the news that the only model available reasonably quickly was finished in quite the wrong colour could throw her off the scent of the car she wanted. A few weeks after the telephone call, M. Savoye drove a Morgan out to Miss Bardot's home in the Bois de Boulogne and she took it for a drive with Gunter Sachs. She is well known for being a competent driver and so, although the car may have felt very strange to her, she got on well with it and bought it. At the time of writing she still has it and, although it is not her regular car, still runs it from time to time.

In general, French Morgan owners are not like the English ones. They are mostly sons of rich families and are generally under thirty years old. But there can be no doubt that Morgan has quite a loyal following abroad. The case of a girl who was a medical student in Paris is typical: she bought a Morgan and ran it for three years and then, deciding that it was too much like hard work, sold it and bought a Lancia. Not long after her new car was delivered, however, she realized that she had been too deeply bitten by the Morgan bug to be able to give them up, so she sold the Lancia and went back to the products of Malvern Link!

No description of the Morgan scene in France would be complete without mentioning M. Jacques Savoye himself, who, as I have said, has been the Paris agent since 1953. In the late 1930s, he raced to very good effect with Le Mans Singers, and although he is now over seventy, he still enters 4/4s in the occasional competition and meets with considerable success.

In Italy, Morgan ownership is slightly different. According to Tino Mattoli, the Rome agent, it is essentially a connoisseur's car there, as it is only connoisseurs who ever get to hear of it. Sig. Mattoli is only allocated just over twenty cars every year. This saddens him slightly, as he already has a waiting list of more than forty people and is sure that with the slightest attempt to publicize the car he could easily sell over two hundred per year. He does have some young customers but most Italian Morgan owners are slightly older professional people and, as in England, a number of doctors and lawyers show very great enthusiasm for it. Spare parts are a slight problem in Italy: as Mattoli only sells twenty cars per year, he is unable to keep a full stock of parts and most items have to be air-freighted from Malvern. This is an expensive business, although it does not seem to bother the Italians unduly.

Mattoli is an agent for Lamborghini as well as Morgan, and so it was rather an embarrassing moment for him when a senior public relations man at the Lamborghini works telephoned to say that Mr. Lamborghini wanted a Morgan immediately. Mattoli explained that he would have to wait a minimum of nine months for the car, but the P.R. man would not accept this. Mattoli therefore telephoned the distribution manager at Malvern who expressed his regret but insisted that there could be no queue-jumping even for so distinguished a man as Mr. Lamborghini. Mattoli accordingly reported this to the P.R. man and the matter appeared to be closed. However, ten minutes later the telephone rang and on the other end of the line was Lamborghini himself. In the best Italian tradition he simply could not believe that a little English company was not prepared to go in for queue-barging. He probably never would have ordered a Morgan after this had it not been for a cancellation from another customer, which enabled Mattoli to offer this car to him. Lamborghini had wanted a two-seater and this was a four-seater; he had wanted a certain colour, this car was black; nevertheless, he accepted it and, I am told, gave it to a friend.

In Germany, the marketing arrangements did not prove at all satisfactory in the 1960s. However, since the appointment of Merz and Pabst in Stuttgart in 1969, the whole sales pattern has changed. Herr Merz introduced the car to the German motoring magazine *Auto Motor und Sport* in May 1970 and, according to the *Financial Times*, received over three hundred inquiries as a result of an article about Morgans which later appeared—inquiries that came not only from Germany but from Romania and Czechoslovakia as well. The result is that Morgan is now beginning to have a really enthusiastic following in Germany for the first time, with demand being infinitely greater than supply.

In America, the Morgan is the answer to the prayer of those who wish to 'escape from mass-production to a haven of craftsmanship and individuality'. The car has probably had (with the exception of 1961–2) a more consistently enthusiastic following in the United States since the war than in any other part of the world, including England. The reaction of *Car and Driver* to the news that Morgans were no longer going to be sold in America, after the federal regulations came into force in 1966, was typical of American affection for Morgans. The magazine printed an obituary of the firm: taking a whole page surrounded by a black border, with a caricature of a Morgan driving away into a forest at night, it printed these words: 'We are consigning the Morgan to history. The last of the great coal carts, a pure antique, and our federal government has sternly decreed it is no longer to be brought to our shores.'

Happily America did not have to mourn the Morgan for long. The company found that it could meet the federal requirements in the Plus-8 and sales began again in the United States after a stoppage of only three years. Many Americans like to run their Morgans in different types of club events, while others discover a real pleasure in ordinary driving which they never knew existed. Very few Americans drive a Morgan as their only car, but then, the one-car family is now something of a rarity in America anyway. The American ownership is really one of the most enthusiastic in the world—Peter Morgan says that he dare not take a stand at the New York Motor Show for fear of being so inundated with orders that he would have to quote delivery dates in 1984!

But Morgan enthusiasm is by no means confined to Europe and America, as this complete list of exports for 1971 shows (figures are approximate, not exact):

Australia	6
Austria	12
Belgium	10
Denmark	4
France	25
Germany	40
Holland	6
Italy	25
Japan	10
New Guinea	4
New Zealand	3
South Africa	6
Spain	2
Sweden	10
Switzerland	12
U.S.A.	40

In addition to these, occasional cars have been sent to Finland, Formosa and the Virgin Islands. Only one is recorded as having been sent to Morocco and that belongs to the King. Another crowned head who is shortly to become a Morgan owner is King Hussein of Jordan, who will have the first Morgan to be exported to his country. Until recently about forty Morgans were sent to Canada each year, but this has temporarily ceased until Morgans can be sure of meeting their recently imposed safety regulations. Thus all the signs are that Morgans are going to become more and more internationally known and that enthusiasm for the marque will soon encompass all parts of the globe.

One very important part of the Morgan scene in the modern world is the club scene. Morgan owners in England have formed groups and clubs since the earliest days but now more and more Morgan clubs are coming into existence in other parts of the world. In England there are two Morgan clubs, each with its own regional centres, and these are the Three-Wheeler Club and the Morgan Sports Car Club (which used to be called the 4/4 Club). There is, on the whole, a strict division of interest between the former, which caters for three-wheelers, and the latter which caters for four-wheelers, yet both groups have enormous enthusiasm and both do a lot of good for the Morgan marque.

The origins of the Three-Wheeler Club may be traced back to the early 1920s, although it was not until 1927 that it really became important.* As was shown in 'The Great Years of the Three-Wheeler', E. B. Ware's crash in 1924 had far-reaching consequences for Morgans in excluding them from club racing. To combat this irritating state of affairs, the Morgan Three-Wheeler Club decided to lift the Morgans-only restriction on ownership and, under the name of the Cyclecar Club (a name which had been used for a while by the Junior Car Club in its earliest days), admitted owners of all makes of cyclecar. The Club adopted the A.C.U. definition of a cyclecar, that is a vehicle not exceeding 8 cwt. in weight and having an engine capacity of not more than 1,100 c.c. It carried out some excellent work in organizing races and competitions for its members who had been deprived of these ever since the Ware crash.

By the early 1930s, a feeling was growing up that there should once again be a Morgan-only club. Thus a Morgan Owners' Club was formed in March 1934, but in the next month it became the Morgan Three-Wheeler Club and the policy was changed to admit all makes of three-wheeler. It was not until 1945 that the present Morgan Three-Wheeler Club was formed, and today it is one of the most successful and well-run vintage car clubs in the world. Some indication of the enthusiasm of its 750 members will become clear when I say that no less than 300 Morgan three-wheelers assembled

* See Brian Watts, *The Three Wheeler* (Morgan Three-Wheeler Club).

Club-member Clarrie Coombes at the wheel of the 1935 Super Sports model he rebuilt for his son

The Morgan clubs in action: celebrating the firm's sixtieth birthday at Prescott, June 1970

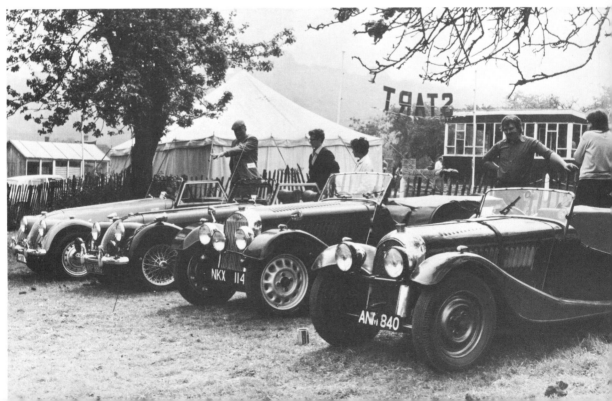

at Prescott in June 1970 to celebrate sixty years of Morgans. The club has a very efficient spare parts organization and, like the Bentley Drivers' Club, has irreplaceable spare parts specially made for it. Also included in its facilities are excellent technical advice and information services.

The other club in England, the Morgan Sports Car Club, was founded in 1951 by a group of enthusiasts in the Derby area and, from small beginnings, has now risen to a total membership of over seven hundred. The club is immensely active, both as a whole and through its regional centres, in organizing all sorts of activities for its members. On the sporting side there are inter-club competitions, sprints, hill-climbs and driving tests, and on the social side there are the famous 'Noggins' and the annual dinner and dance. When a pub is selected by a regional centre for a Noggin, one bar is usually set aside for club members, who come from all over the district to 'talk Morgans' and to get together over a drink, and sometimes there are film or slide shows. The annual dinner of the club is always an exciting event and is often attended by more than two hundred people. It is at this event that the club's trophies are presented for such things as best performance of the year in a Plus-4, best performance in a Plus-8, best performance by a lady driver and so forth.

As the Morgan Sports Car Club is only interested in four-wheelers, most of its members' cars are more modern than those belonging to Three-Wheeler Club members and, consequently, the spare-parts problem is not so serious. Nevertheless, the club has begun to organize a spares register which will, with the passing of time, become increasingly useful to members who own early models.

Other highly enthusiastic clubs exist in America in the Washington area and in California, in Australia, South Africa and New Zealand, as well as an outpost of the British Three-Wheeler Club in New Jersey, U.S.A. Plans are also being made, I understand, to start a club in New Zealand.

All these clubs play a most valuable role: on the practical side they help to build up a store of knowledge on how to maintain Morgans and how to obtain parts easily where there are no local service facilities. Furthermore, the clubs ensure that both Morgans and Morgan enthusiasm is known all over the world. They ensure that the Morgan is a 'sports car' in the active sense of the word, and not just something that is called a 'sports car' but which is never entered in any competition.

There is certainly something remarkable about the

Morgan in this modern world. Ownership of one or even general enthusiasm for the marque creates a unique link between people. It is a healthy, sporting, friendly car and these characteristics seem to be reflected in the personalities of the people who like it. Two Morgan enthusiasts meeting for the first time feel as though they have been friends for life in less than five minutes. One only has to observe the frantic waving and headlight flashing that goes on when two Morgans pass each other on the roads to understand what a remarkable *ésprit de corps* exists among all those who like them—actually the three-wheeler drivers have to be a little careful not to overdo the light-flashing in case they run their batteries flat! No other currently produced car has such a remarkable effect on people. Of course not. The Morgan is unique.

The Future

The Morgan Motor Company has now been in existence for over sixty years and we have seen in 'The Business History' how it has gone through many ups and downs. As Peter Morgan himself says, the company's greatest achievement lay not in making a car that could cover 60 miles in one hour in 1912, but in surviving so many decades of change. At the moment the company is in an extremely healthy state, with a good international market and a very enthusiastic following throughout the world. What, then, does the future hold in store? Let us look first at how the car itself will develop.

Morgan says that he sees the car keeping its present style for some time to come. He does not suggest that it is just right as it is, and acknowledges that the older he gets the more he notices shortcomings in the car's comfort: yet, although he drives an absolutely standard Plus-8, he loves it.

Although the 1930s-type styling is here to stay, at least for the foreseeable future, it is possible that a time will come when some of the Morgan's 'thirties feel' will have to go. This very much depends on Morgan owners; if it becomes clear that an altogether 'softer' car is wanted, the factory will have to oblige, but I for one hope that this will not happen.

The faithful old Morgan front suspension is also here to stay for the foreseeable future. This suspension is perhaps the company's greatest engineering triumph, for no other system has been in constant use for so long nor has shown itself so adaptable to great variations in engine size. Criticisms are sometimes made, but one of its qualities is quite undeniable—its strength. When Peter Morgan goes in for trials, his car receives the most appalling battering, yet the suspension never fails him and this makes him rightly reluctant to think about changing it.

ED FRANKLIN

MY HEART BELONGS TO MORGAN

Cartoon from the Canadian newspaper, The Globe

On the business side, all the indications are that the potential world market for the car is constantly expanding, and so far the company has not had too much difficulty in meeting safety requirements and specifications laid down by foreign governments. One factor which is helping the potential market to expand is the great improvement in the quality of roads in many parts of the globe. A certain minimum standard of road surface is certainly a factor taken into account by those who are considering investing in a Morgan! The advent of the Common Market, too, should put the company in a still stronger position in Europe and, in the meantime, new agencies are opening up in the most surprising places, one of the most recent being Tahiti. During a visit to England, the wife of the man who wanted to sell Morgans in Tahiti adorned many of the senior staff at Malvern with garlands, and perhaps this helped to secure the agency for her husband!

Peter Morgan would like the works to be enlarged; but don't get worried—whatever happens he has no intention of even approaching the thousand-car-per-year mark. People usually suppose that he doesn't want to make more cars but this in fact is not true. He does try to make more cars each year, since, if he didn't, turnover would go down instead of remaining constant as it has now for some years. Fifteen or twenty years ago, he thought that the end of the firm would be brought about when mass-produced rivals priced Morgans out of the market, but so far this hasn't happened, although the possibility remains and is one of the factors that worries him most. He would never want to go in for large-scale production and will be absolutely content if the annual output eventually reaches the 750 mark.

Morgans are quite ready to re-equip the works with any machinery necessary to produce the car as it is now or as it may be in the future, but Peter does not envisage very large-scale re-equipping. He finds it possible to buy more and more ready-made components, which can be more cheaply produced by a specialist outside firm making tens of thousands than by Morgans themselves. The example of wheel-nuts is an obvious one. Every Plus-8 requires 25 of these, which adds up to 6,250 nuts per year. A manufacturer producing vast quantities of wheel-nuts can sell this number to Morgans far more cheaply than they could make them at Malvern. It is therefore possible that a slightly smaller proportion of the car will be Malvern-made in the future, but this will not lead to a falling-off in quality. The Morgan is such an unconventional car that the factory will always have plenty of work to do. Even for 750 cars per year, it would never be worthwhile getting Pressed Steel to tool up to make body panels—they will always have to be made by hand.

Peter Morgan is also not ignoring the possibility that his firm may one day produce an electric car. As Morgans have never produced their own engine this would, of course, be dependent on having access to someone else's power unit. But if the world was tending towards electric cars and a good motor were available, he would be quite open to the idea of using it while preserving the general appearance of the car. No doubt Morgans would be able to continue their policy of producing cars with a high power-to-weight unit even if they were powered by batteries, for the car would still remain that much lighter than most of its competitors. However, it is difficult to see electric cars becoming at all widespread until the battery as we know it today has been revolutionized.

For Peter Morgan, the satisfaction in his work lies chiefly in meeting the challenge of trying to build motor cars. It is a challenge that he has enjoyed enormously, and one that he has met with great success, and so there is very little likelihood of his withdrawing from the firm until he is well past the retiring age. But what will happen then? Peter has a son, Charles, now in his early twenties, who would appear to be the obvious successor. No one can say if he really will take over the firm, as the motor world is changing all the time, but he is a young man with all the best qualities of the Morgan family in him. He is very fond of cars and takes a keen interest in design and styling. Like his grandfather he is a great individualist and so, if he finds a realistic challenge in the motor industry, I think the chances are that he will take it up.

The face of the future: Charles Morgan in the Land's End trial, 1970

Index